MARTIAL

ARTS

OR

SCIENCE?

First edition

Aviraj Sinha & Yashraj Sinha

Warm Wishes

Aviraj
Sinha

Yashraj
Sinha

ACKNOWLEDGEMENT

First, I would like to acknowledge all the people who led me on my journey to writing this book; to everyone who supported, taught, worked, and took care of me.

Through this book I would like to express the knowledge passed on to me by all my past instructors, specifically all instructors from Master Lofton of Lofton's fighting Tigers and Ms. Carol Frentz's of American Taekwondo Association (ATA) of Katy.

I especially thank my family who aided me in research. Without them I would never have been set on the path of a martial artist and definitely would not have been able to write this book.

Lastly, I would also like to thank all the other martial artists who did this research before me and who I stand on the shoulders of.

ABOUT THE AUTHORS

Aviraj Sinha (Avi) is a freshman at Southern Methodist University (SMU) pursuing majors in Computer Science and Business. Avi graduated from Seven Lakes high school with academic distinction. Avi started martial arts when he was 9 years old and has been practicing it since. He earned his 1st degree black belt under the guidance of Master Lofton in Shorin Ryu and also earned his 2nd degree black belt in Songham, Taekwondo from ATA, Katy. The author was also a member of the leadership class and has instructed junior martial artists. Avi has won multiple trophies at various levels. He has also been awarded ATA national scholarship in 2015. He is also an accomplished clarinet player and has received high ratings at state and regional events. He has also represented Seven lakes High School marching band at state completion. The author's parents are in the computer profession and work as consultants.

Yashraj Sinha (Yash) is a sophomore at Seven Lakes High school with a goal to become either a computer scientist or a physicist. He was introduced to martial arts when he was 5 years old and has been practicing martial arts since then. He has earned his 1st degree black belt under the guidance of Master Lofton in Shorin Ryu and also earned his 2nd degree black belt in Songham, Taekwondo from ATA, Katy. The author is a member of the leadership team at the ATA academy and has instructed junior martial artists. Yash is also an ardent sportsman and loves playing tennis. He had represented BDJH in junior high tennis and has also won placements in USTA open tournaments. The author is a gifted clarinet players and has won regional and state placement as a solo artists and in ensemble. He is also a member of award winning SLHS marching band.

The author's parents are in the computer profession and work as consultants.

TABLE OF CONTENTS

PREFACE

My experience started with the lack of social interaction in my life, which disconcerted my parents; after great discussion they encouraged me to take up Karate classes in Memphis, TN. Fortunately, my Karate instructor had a passion for martial arts that found its way to me. The fact that he was the first person to introduce me to the concept of sportsmanship, helped me achieve a higher level of seriousness that allowed me to shine at tournaments and boost my self-confidence.

For 7 years, I rapidly rose in the ranks by winning tournaments and testing; eventually, I reached the black belt level in Shorin Ryu when I was fifteen. Along with this new sense of pride came additional duties: mentoring my colored-belt peers. Experimenting with ways to spread my distinctive understanding of martial arts to them, I organized martial arts into an informative guide, as a pure, objective science. I believe my understanding of the underlying philosophy of programming allowed me to realize that in the same way programs are made up of primitive variables, martial arts are related to the concept of physics (energy and force), knowledge of human anatomy (bone density, key organs, impact zone) and power of mind (Psychology and Concentration).

This book will look at martial arts beyond what the naked eye can see. It will give you the historical data amassed from over thousands of years, an understanding of the biological weapon of your own body, and the physical properties that allow one to win in martial arts. Considering this division of martial arts, the book is divided into these various subject areas: Art and Science (biological, psychological, physical).

Though the book may not make you a martial artist, it will give a new view of martial arts and remove unscientific misconceptions. It will teach the overarching view of martial arts as a whole rather than a narrow-biased sample. Overall, I want to show that martial arts are more than a competitive art; they are the empirical evidence amassed over thousands of years of research, trial, and error.

PART 1
MARTIAL ARTS

CHAPTER 1- INTRODUCTION: OVERVIEW OF MARTIAL ARTS

Before understanding the term Martial arts, let's get an insight of the times when there were no nuclear weapons or fatal bombs and the only means of battle were other forms of fights including striking, self-defense and in whole martial arts. The term Martial arts is derived from the Latin word Art of Mars, in which Mars was the god of war. Early Roman mythology believe Mars to be the harbinger of peace and tranquility. He was not a destructive agent but more of a military power that brings about peace. So the name became Martial arts.

Centuries ago, as far back as in 15th century, the practice of martial arts emerged in ancient Europe and North Asian parts of the country including China. The historical traces can be dated back to Mongolian era where Martial arts were evolving and traces of their prevalence were found. If we ruffle the pages of the Ancient history there are stories of numerous historical battles that were fought on the lines of Martial arts. They are the oldest forms of fighting. There are sculptures depicting the battlers with in martial style and people practicing the art. Historians have predicted that at those times, martial arts emerged from the wars, and historical texts stand for its authenticity.

Historians have found various stones and traces of dragon symbols in the Mongolian and ancient Europe in the 15th-16th century and that goes a long way in establishing the existence of martial arts. The dragon is known to be a symbol of power and is synonymous to the martial arts. It can be associated with many modern forms of Martial arts like Kung Fu.

Martial arts have since then evolved and come of age. From the 15th century to the 21st century, there have been vast changes and evolution of martial arts. Though the basic forms remain the same, there are numerous changes with the lapse of time. There are various styles and forms that we will be studying. To get a detailed knowledge of the Martial arts, we will first have to understand why there was a sudden upsurge in the martial arts. Martial arts not only stand for battles, power, and war but are synonymous to a strong willpower, a balanced mind, and a calmness of the body. Martial arts have multiplied today in terms of forms and people who follow it ethically but there were always similar reasons for its tremendous growth. Before moving ahead, let's understand the reasons underlying for the growth of martial arts over the period of time.

For self-defense

With the onset of wars and battles all around the globe and the spread of violence everywhere, there was a strong need to combat aggression on an individual level. To safeguard one's dignity and personal safety, one needed to be well trained in the skills of self-defense and self-reliance. There were various forms of martial arts that helped attain this goal. The main reason for the growth of martial arts can be attributed to the fact that it contains self-defense techniques that act as a personal guard. It can be applied at any time and in all the real time scenarios. People have different needs and reasons for practicing martial arts and each could differ. For some it might be a sport or it can be a fitness regime, but in today's world it has proved its relevance as a self-defense method. Depending upon the situation, any of the forms such as Kick boxing, Judo and Karate can be applied in real scenario. Training may initially be hard work but it eventually pays off over time. There are a large number of trainers and physical education classes that work towards the creation of a pool of martial arts followers.

Spirituality oriented

Martial arts require the practitioner to be mentally strong and have a firm will power. Not only does it tame the hostility but it makes one spiritually inclined. It tends to reduce the aggression within the mind rather than use it as a deprecating tool, to use it as a means of achieving state of peace by alleviating negative forces. Martial arts are at times associated with Buddhism. There are documented evidences and a school of thought that believes that both have similar concepts of mental stability, peaceful thoughts and actions that similarly involve the elimination of any kind of aggressive attacks. Although it is difficult to state whether Buddhist monks were trained physically, there are people who say that both martial arts and Buddhism when it reached China, were followed by the same people. There are sects of Zen Buddhists who are believed to be trained in Martial arts but there is still some confusion with terms of written evidence.

Alternative for fatal war techniques

Martial arts are more of a self-defense and a non-fatal way to battle than other techniques that could be life endangering. War techniques completely does away with dependency on massive, destructive weapons and makes one self-reliant. It is the power within that is fueled by the oil of willpower and determination to use it for your own benefit.

Physical fitness

Martial arts work by physically strengthening one's body. It's the body that takes the entire toll on itself and therefore it requires maintaining its strength. Once you start practicing martial arts, your body and soul must be healthy. Fatigue, lack of stamina, and ill physical caliber can be overcome by practicing martial arts. As a form of art, it aims at giving holistic benefits to the body and mind. But what happens when the aggression and negative vibes pent up inside us? It tends to burst inside us and destroy us. By practicing martial arts, we tend to vent out the ill vibes and negative thoughts through our body. Our bodies basically get ready to accept positivity from all over. Martial arts cannot be restricted to the study of combat methods only and must include the study of interplay of mind and body.

These reasons led to growth of martial arts and with evolution of arts came in different style and kinds of martial arts which were different from each other yet very similar in its basics.

History of Martial Arts

We read earlier that traces of martial arts in the history can be seen in the form of symbols and pictures carved on stones and sculptures. The pictures depicted people in struggling scenes or with fierce body language. These pictures were found as early as the 3rd and 4th century in the Mesopotamian civilization. In some North Asian countries, paintings were found in which the use of sticks, bows, spears were shown indicating the presence of armed martial arts.

The Chinese martial arts are said to be the oldest and emerged somewhere in Xia dynasty and contains the most prominent and earliest signs of martial arts. However, Europe is also said to be the land of the earliest sources of forms of martial arts such as boxing and wrestling. A number of manuals and pictorials have been in existence since ancient times which authenticates the extensive research done on martial arts during that era.

Evolution in the last century

In the 19th century and early 20th century, martial arts went through an important reform of some kind. It has become more of a modern sport and people around the world started practicing it religiously. Earlier it was just a traditional form of battle whereas now it is developing and assimilating into a modern culture. With the introduction of boxing and fencing as modern sports, the martial arts were going through a change. In and around the same time, Europe, Western nations, and Asian countries realized the importance of martial arts.

One major reform at that time was that military personnel were beginning to teach the military arts as part of their training. It became an inevitable part of the training session, in which the goal was mainly to boost mental and physical fitness as well as to teach self-defense.

Techniques of Martial arts

There are variations within many Martial arts and can be categorized on the following basis:

1. Style

There are historical as well as contemporary/modern styles which are recognized.

2. Region

Martial arts can be attributed to either eastern or western origin which can be further divided within countries.

3. Application

Application is a very important criterion. It can be used for self-defense, combat, or aggression. It depends on the situation in which the practitioner has to apply the art. Sometimes all you need is to just defend yourself without being aggressive. But sometimes it becomes important to give it back to where combat styles come into picture.

Martial arts can further be divided on the basis of techniques.

- Unarmed techniques which include grappling, kicking, punching, boxing, throwing. Judo, Karate and Kung Fu require the use of only limbs and usually restricts the use of any form of a weapon, like a bo or a spear.

- Armed techniques, which involve the use of weapons, are mainly found in Chinese tradition. Its traces were found in historical European martial arts. There were pictorial evidences showing the use of arrows, bows, spears and people aiming at others with full aggression. Today, the armed form of fighting has vanished and the unarmed form is in prevalence. However, they are still not only dangerous but also fatal.

CHAPTER 2- ORIGINS OF MARTIAL ARTS

Martial art or "art of fighting" comes as a natural instinct to human beings. Defending from aggression or attacking enemies has been prevalent since recorded time and has been chronicled in artworks of ancient Egypt. For example, the poems of struggles in Mesopotamia dating back to 3000 BC and the dug drawings from 2879 BC instructing the combat of spears, swords, sticks, and bows depict how these ancient struggles use of martial arts to prevent it. The term "martial arts" today is typically tantamount to "Asian fighting arts" as most popular martial arts finds their origin from Asian cultures.

2.1 Asia

India

Martial arts are a part of India's ancient culture and traditional games. Elements of yoga which focuses on understating the strength of body and used strength of focus in ways of meditation was root source of Indian martial arts philosophy. Indian martial arts have an important influence in the development of modern Asian martial arts. Spread of Indian theology led it to spread its ways of yoga in martial arts to surrounding countries such as Vietnam, Thailand, Laos, Malaysia, Cambodia, parts of China, etc. Predating the Indo-Aryan migrations, the oldest martial art found in South Asia is *Mallayuddha* -basic form of combat wrestling that includes "barbaric" features such as knee strikes to the chest, punches to the head, and hair pulling.

China

Record of Chinese martial arts can be traced to the Xia Dynasty; its origin is attributed to self-defense needs, hunting activities, and military training in ancient China. Similar movements of the Mudra hand positions in Hinduism, Buddhism, and the Chinese shaolin style suggest an important influence of Indian practices on Chinese martial arts. By the 16th and 17th centuries, not only did monks of Shaolin practice martial arts, but martial practice had become such an integral element of Shaolin monastic life that the monks felt the need to justify it by creating new Buddhist lore. From the turmoil of the Japanese invasion and the Chinese Civil War, Chinese martial arts became more accessible to the general public as many martial artists were encouraged to openly teach their art. In today's society, Chinese martial arts are an integral element of Chinese culture.

Japan

Martial arts in Japan date back in history to medieval times when they were first born of a need to prepare for combat and protection. Although most of the martial arts were influenced from Chinese martial arts, they vastly differ in style. Japanese martial arts involve straight-line attacks, whereas Chinese techniques are more circular. In addition, the martial arts of Japan have a wide range starting from empty hand-to-hand techniques, to fighting with several weapons. It was mainly practiced by samurai since they were chosen warriors whose duties were to protect the nobility.

These fighting arts were gradually modified by the Japanese over time. Two sections of Japanese martial arts were created: Traditional school (*Koryu*) and modern martial way (*Gendai budo*). Traditional school contains Sumo (wrestling), Jujutsu (redirection), swordsmanship (katana) and Ninjutsu (assassin). Modern martial arts contain Judo (redirection), Aikido (harmony with ki), and Karate (empty hand).

Korea

Korean Martial Arts have two thousand years of history and an abundance of forms. The oldest form of martial arts in Korea was *sireum* (a type of wrestling) used to train soldiers, but it became popular among villagers during festivals, celebrations, acrobatics, and sport.

Modern styles are practiced largely across the globe and are probably the most recognizable cultural aspect of Korea. Of all the Korean Martial Arts, Taekwondo is undeniably the most popular. In 2000, it became an Olympic sport making its debut at the Sydney 2000 Olympic Games. Korean martial arts are largely characterized by self-defense, discipline, unity, balance, and control; but with over 25 forms being in practice today, there is a lot of variety in style and technique. The roots of many can be found in Chinese and Japanese martial arts as they have evolved into a uniquely Korean art form.

2.2 Africa

The earliest evidence of martial arts as practiced in Africa 3,400 years B.C. comes from depiction of fight in the hieroglyphics on the walls of Egyptian tombs in the ancient temples of Karnak. Every nation, or "tribe" in Africa, has its own complex and complete martial arts styles that can be seen all over the world.

Africa contains 3 main sections of martial arts: bare knuckle boxing, stick-fighting, and folk wrestling. Stick-fighting uses simple long slender, blunt, hand-held, generally wooden 'sticks' for fighting: such as a staff, cane, walking stick, baton, etc. Most cultures have developed regional forms of grappling in folk wrestling. Africa contains *Lucha canaria* (style of wrestling originating from the Canary Island), *Lutte Traditionolle* (traditional wrestling), *Tigel* (Ethiopian), and *Grech* (Tunisian). Bare wrestling is also classified as a regional martial art. Dambe is a form of boxing found in West Africa and is usually classified as a striking art.

2.3 Europe

Although Europe has little surviving links to ancient martial arts, some combat manuals and documents dating from the late middle ages to the early modern period help explain the style of European martial arts. These include ancient Greek wrestling and gladiatorial combat.

European martial arts became more prominent with *Pankration* and other martially oriented disciplines of the Ancient Olympics. Boxing became an Olympic sport in Greece as early as 688 BC. Gladiatorial combat is documented form the Colosseum in Rome from the 260s BC, and the Icelandic sagas contain many realistic stories of Viking Age combat.

2.4 Timeline

Key milestones in martial art history are listed below:

Prehistoric:

2000BC – Murals in tomb 15 at Beni Hasan, depicting wrestling techniques.

800BC – Start of Greek Olympic Competition introducing martial arts like boxing, wrestling, and *pankration* flourished.

800BC – Homer's Iliad's description of hand-to-hand combat in detail.

400BC – Indian scriptures (Vedas) mentions South Asian martial arts such as Boxing, wrestling, swordsmanship, archery, and the use of numerous weapons are all described in detail.

264 BC – First recorded gladiatorial combat in Rome.

50 BC – Earliest records of a Korean martial art.

72 AD – The Coliseum opens in Rome, providing the public with the world's largest martial arts venue for over the next three hundred years.

100 AD – Buddhist texts such as the Lotus Sutra mention a number of South Asian fighting arts.

477 AD –Shaolin Temple introduces martial arts in the monastery.

1200 AD – Japanese samurai class emerges.

Modern period:

1600 AD – Samurai sword, called a katana got popular.

1700 AD –Shaolin monks combat style gain popularity

1892 – The first world heavyweight boxing championship is fought.

1900 –Japanese martial got introduced to west

1908 – Amateur boxing becomes an Olympic Sport.

1935 – "Karate" becomes official name of the Okinawan martial arts.

1943 – Judo, Karate, and various Chinese systems are officially introduced in Korea, likely beginning to mix with the indigenous Korean arts.

1959 – Bruce Lee arrives in America and begins to teach Chinese martial arts.

1964 – Judo becomes an official Olympic sport

1966 – International Taekwondo Federation (ITF) is formed.

2000- Taekwondo debuts in Sydney Olympics

CHAPTER 3- MODERN MARTIAL ARTS

Traditional martial arts -which originated in Asia- included physical, mental and spiritual codes. Western combative sports like boxing, wrestling, and fencing were, in contrast, with more physical and technical aspects. Over time, both styles have cross pollinated to produce a fusion version of martial arts. This fusion includes the philosophy of traditional martial arts (Asian) and the military application of western martial art.

3.1 Growth of modern martial arts

The global interest in Asian martial arts and newly formed combative sports arises towards the end of the 19th century due to the increase in relations between the western world with China and Japan. As Europe was developing the rules of boxing and fencing as sports, Japan was giving final touches to the modern forms of Judo, Jujutsu, Karate, and Kendo. These

3 first became popular among the mainstream from the 1950s-60s, due in part to Asian and Hollywood martial arts movies.

Bruce Lee is credited as one of the first instructors to openly teach Chinese martial arts to Westerners. World Judo Championships have been held since 1956, and Judo was introduced to the Summer Olympics in 1964. Karate World Championships were introduced in 1970. Asian martial arts experienced a surge of popularity in the west during the 1970s resulting in numerous coaching schools.

3.2 Martial Arts in Olympics

Ancient Olympics started in 776 BC with wrestling being contested as early as 708 BC, boxing in 688 BC, chariot racing in 680 BC, and *Pankration*- a combination of boxing and wrestling- in 648 BC. Physical combat had made up a large portion of the events in ancient Olympics and had few rules unlike today's modern events, resulting in a more aggressive nature.

Modern Olympics started in 1896 with 9 sports and 43 events and was hosted in Athens, Greece. Boxing has been practiced since the 1904 Olympic Games and boxing for women since the 2012 Games. Taekwondo was part of the Olympic Games in 1992 and 1996 as an exhibition sport. It debuted officially at the 2000 Games for men and women. Judo has been present since the 1964 Games (except for 1968) and since the 1992 Games for women. Greco-Roman Wrestling is included as sport since the first Games in 1896. Women don't compete in

Greco-roman.Freestyle Wrestling has been an olympic sport since 1904 Games. Womens freestyle was added in 2004.Fencing has also been part of the olympic program since the first Games in 1896 and for women since the 1924 Games. The Summer Olympic Games now includes Judo, Taekwondo, western archery, boxing, javelin, wrestling and fencing as events.

3.3 Popular martial arts

There are many popular martial arts around the world. I have listed few which are prominent and are universally recognized and practiced.

Aikido

Aikido was based on an ancient Japanese system of self-defense. Aikido techniques consist of entering and turning movements that redirect the momentum of an opponent's attack, and a throw or joint lock that terminates the technique. Unlike some other martial art forms, in which force is met with counter-force, aikido employs the technique of avoiding action by making use of an opponent's forward impetus, causing the attacker to suffer a temporary loss of balance.

Aikido was among the first martial arts freed from the ban imposed on their practice by the US government after

World War II. In some areas, Japanese police officers are required to hold at least a *Shodan* (black belt) in Aikido.

Jiu-Jitsu

Jiu-Jitsu uses hand-to-hand combat method mainly as an unarmed self-defense. The roots of Jujitsu lie in sumo, which has a long history. Jujitsu techniques include kicking, striking, kneeing, throwing, choking, joint locking, holding, and tying, as well as use of certain weapons. It was developed to defeat armored samurai in hand-to-hand combat or a short weapon. Jujitsu was always a secondary method of combat to the warrior, since he relied so heavily on his sword. These techniques were developed around the principle of using an attacker's energy against him, rather than directly opposing it.

Brazilian Jiu-Jitsu is a martial art, combat sport, and a self-defense system that focuses on grappling and especially ground fighting. BJJ promotes the concept that a smaller, weaker person can successfully defend against a bigger, stronger assailant by using proper technique, leverage, and most notably, taking the fight to the ground, and then applying joint-locks and chokeholds to defeat the opponent.

Judo

Judo meaning "gentle way" is a martial art that originated in Japan, and it is now known around the world as an Olympic sport. Judo was established in 1882 by combining Jujitsu with mental discipline. Its most prominent feature is its competitive element, where the objective is to either throw or takedown an opponent to the ground, immobilize, or otherwise subdue an opponent with a pin or force an opponent to submit with a joint lock or a choke. Strikes and thrusts by hands and feet as well as weapons defenses are a part of Judo, but only in pre-arranged forms are weapons allowed in Judo competition or free practice. A Judo practitioner is called a Judoka. There are three basic categories of *waza* (technique) in Judo: *nage-waza*, *katame-waza* and *atemi-waza*.

Karate

Karate, the Japanese word for "empty hand," was born in the Okinawan Islands as a form of self-defense, at a time when weapons were banned by invading Japanese forces. It began as *te* (hand), a fighting style used by the natives of the Ryukyu Islands, and was later influenced by Chinese families that settled on Okinawa after trade relationships between China and the islands were established. Although the origin of this is not well documented but the scholars believe that that it came from India over a thousand years ago, brought to China by a Buddhist monk named *Bodhidarma*.

Karate is predominantly a striking art using punching, kicking, knee strikes, elbow strikes and open hand techniques such as knife-hands, spear-hands, and palm-heel strikes. Historically and in some modern styles grappling, throws, joint locks, restraints, and vital point strikes are also taught. A Karate practitioner is called a *Karateka*.

Boxing

The earliest evidence of boxing dates back to Egypt around 3000 BC. The sport was introduced to the ancient Olympic Games by the Greeks in the late 7th century BC. Boxing is a martial art and combat sport in which two people throw punches at each other, usually with gloved hands. The goals have been to weaken and knock down the opponent. Amateur boxing is both an Olympic and Commonwealth sport and is a common fixture in most international games—it also has its own World Championships.

Boxing made Olympic debut at the 1904 Games in St Louis, women's boxing made its debut at the 2012 London Games in London.

Kung Fu

Kung-Fu is the most ancient of all martial arts with its roots in China tracing back to more than 4,000 years. Adapted from Indian yoga postures, the earliest form of Chinese martial arts was those practiced by soldiers for direct use in battlefield combat. Shaolin Kung Fu is based on the characteristics and attack methods of more than a dozen different animals, including the snake, the tiger, the dragon and the cobra. Shaolin monks in China incorporated the exercise forms with their philosophy of nonviolence, using Kung Fu only as a form of self-defense. Strengthening the thighs, improving balance and exercises that enhance perception, precision and speed are valuable attributes that can be applied to each different style of Shaolin Kung Fu.

Kung Fu gained popularity in early 1900's especially in China, where competitions were held throughout China. In 1936 Kung-Fu was put on the world stage at the Berlin Olympic Games.

Muay Thai

Muay Thai is a national combat sport of Thailand, which uses stand-up striking along with various clinching techniques. It was developed several hundreds of years ago as a form of close-combat that utilizes the entire body as a weapon. Muay Thai is referred to as "The Art of Eight Limbs"; and using eight points of contact the body mimics weapons of war. The hands become the sword and dagger; the shins and forearms were hardened in training to act as armor against blows, and the elbow to fell opponents like a heavy mace or hammer; the legs and knees became the axe and staff. The body operated as one unit. The knees and elbows constantly searching and testing for an opening while grappling and trying to spin an enemy to the ground for the kill.

Today, the blocks and strikes of Muay Thai are often seen in the kickboxing ring. Muay Thai became widespread internationally in the twentieth century, and gained popularity with MMA adopting many of its techniques.

Taekwondo

Tae Kwon Do is the art of self-defense that originated in Korea. It is recognized as one of the oldest forms of martial arts in the world, reaching back over 2,000 years. The name was selected for its appropriate description of the art: Tae (foot), Kwon (hand), Do (art).Taekwondo martial art with a heavy emphasis on kicks, such as tornado kick and spinning hook kick.

Tae Kwon Do first gained acceptance as an Olympic sport when it appeared as a demonstration event in the 1988 Seoul Olympic Games. Tae Kwon Do became a full medal sport competition beginning in 2000 at the Sydney Olympics.

Tai Chi

Tai chi is an internal Chinese martial art practiced for both its defense training and its health benefits. Tai Chi, also known as Shadow Boxing, is one of the major branches of the traditional Chinese martial arts. The essential principles of Tai Chi are based on the ancient Chinese philosophy of Taoism, which stresses the natural balance in all things and the need for living in spiritual and physical accord with the patterns of nature. Modern day Tai Chi was developed around 1670 and is characterized by contrasting and complimentary movements-slow and soft versus fast and hard. It contains explosive power and low stances. Chen style is more difficult and physically demanding than Sun style; thus it is not the best style to start with if you have arthritis.

Wrestling

Wrestling is one of the oldest forms of combat depicted in 5000-year-old sculptures in Sumer. For the Greeks, wrestling was a science and a divine art, and it represented the most important training for young men. Always popular in ancient Greece, wrestling held a prominent place in the Olympic Games. It was developed by ancient Greeks as a way to train soldiers in hand-to-hand combat. During the Ancient Olympic Games, from 708 B.C., wrestling was the decisive discipline of the *Pentathlon*.

Wrestling is a combat sport involving grappling type techniques such as clinch fighting, throws and takedowns, joint locks, pins and other grappling holds. A wrestling bout is a physical competition, between two (occasionally more) competitors or sparring partners, who attempt to gain and maintain a superior position. There are a wide range of styles with varying rules with both traditional historic and modern styles. Wrestling techniques have been incorporated into other martial arts as well as military hand-to-hand combat systems.

In 1904, freestyle wrestling was first introduced during the St. Louis Olympic Games. Female wrestling as an Olympic discipline was introduced in Athens Games in 2004. Traditional and modern forms of wrestling are practiced on every continent and in almost every country.

3.4 Techniques

Martial arts primarily started as a fighting art thus the techniques reflect the spirit of fighting. Martial arts techniques can be divided in 3 types:

Empty hand technique- Techniques such as strikes, kicks …etc. falls in this category. In this the fighter uses his body only for defense and offense.

Weaponry technique –Techniques involve using different weapons such as sword, knife, sticks…etc.

Calming technique- These softer techniques such as *Chi*, meditation …etc. is used to enhance mental sharpness.

Punches and Strikes

Use of punches and strikes are very fundamental to most forms of martial arts. A basic punch is a striking blow with the closed fist and is used in some martial arts and combat sports, most notably boxing. The use of punches varies between different martial arts and combat sports. Styles such as boxing use punches alone, while martial art such as Karate use punches along with kicks. Others such as wrestling and Judo do not use punches at all.

Strikes in Karate are mainly thrust punches using the knuckles, the palm, or the side of the hand, while strikes in Shaolin Kungfu can be made not only with a fist but also with other hand forms like the tiger-claw or the leopard punch. The punch techniques in Muay Thai were originally quite limited being crosses and a long circular strike made with a straight (but not locked) arm.

There are many types of punches and as a result, different styles encompass varying types of punching techniques.

The **hammer-fist** is a closed fist that is brought down upon the target, usually using the side of the hand or wrist. The hammer-fist is effective for striking the temples, the nose, sternum or the top of the head.

A **reverse punch** is a striking blow with the closed fist. The arm is mostly extended with a slight bent in the elbow to prevent injury. Reverse punches hit with the two big knuckles on the hand for maximum damage.

The **uppercut** is a punch that travels along a vertical line at the opponent's chin or solar plexus. Uppercuts are useful when thrown at close range, because they are considered to cause more  damage and also because of the element of surprise.

 The **palm heel** is a strike using the palm of the hand. Whether the hand is open or the fingertips are folded against the bottom knuckles, palm strikes hit with the bottom part of the palm, where the hand meets the wrist. The bottom ridge of the palm is a surprisingly solid striking surface, and can do just as much damage as a closed fist when utilized properly.

An **elbow strike** is a strike with the point of the elbow, the part of the forearm nearest to the elbow, or the part of the upper arm nearest to the elbow. Elbows can be thrown sideways  similarly to a hook, upwards similarly to an uppercut, downwards, diagonally, or in direct movement- like during a jump. Although most martial arts limit the use of elbow strikes, in Muay Thai it is commonly practiced.

Kicks

The use of kicks are a very potent mechanism of offense as well as defense. If properly executed it can be very damaging for the opponent. Kicks are main offensive form used in Muay Thai. Two kinds are primarily used, the *thip* (foot jab) and the roundhouse kick. The Thai roundhouse kick uses a rotational movement of the entire body and has been widely adopted by practitioners of other combat sports. The foot-thrust or literally "foot jab" is mainly used as a defensive technique to control distance or block attacks. Foot-thrusts should be thrown quickly but yet with enough force to knock an opponent off balance.

Taekwondo practitioners utilize both the heel and ball of the foot for striking.

A **round kick** (also known as swinging kick or a power angle kick but often confused with the roundhouse kick) is a kick in which the attacker swings his or her leg around in a semicircular motion, striking with the front of the leg or foot (ball or instep). This type of kick is

utilized in many different martial arts and is popular-such as Karate, Muay Thai, and Taekwondo-in both non-contact and full-contact martial arts competitions. The kick has many variations based on stance, leg movement, striking surface, and the height of the kick.

The **hook kick** strikes with the heel from the side and is executed similar to a side kick. The user uses his/her hamstrings to "hook" the opponent or cause more damage. The hook kick is also used as a fast but powerful counter attack on incoming kicks.

Flying kicks are commonly practiced in Taekwondo, Karate, Wushu, and Muay Thai for fitness, exhibitions, competition, as well as self-defense. It requires the user to jump forward while extending a side kick. This allows the momentum of the body to produce more power.

The **front kick** in martial arts is a kick executed by lifting the knee straight forward, and extended by using quadriceps and hitting with the ball of the foot. The Front kick is routinely used in Karate or Taekwondo.

In **crescent kick**, the leg is bent like the front kick, but the knee is pointed to the left or right of the target. The energy from the snap is then redirected, whipping the leg into an arc and hitting the target from the side. In many styles of Tai chi, crescent kicks are taught as tripping techniques.

The **knee strike** is a basic technique yet it yields a lot of power. The attacker folds their knee up (less than 90 angle) and uses the quadriceps and body momentum to strike the opponent in the head, stomach, or groin. This can cause a knockout or the  opponent to double over. This is commonly found in contact sports such as Muay Thai and boxing.

Throws

A throw is a grappling technique that involves a rotational force to off-balance or lift an opponent and then throwing them to the ground. The practitioner performing the throw releases the opponent and ends up balanced and on their feet as opposed to a takedown where both finish on the ground.

There are several major types of throw among Asian martial arts. Judo is most notably known for its intricate throws and its vast number of throws. Unlike most martial arts, Karate's throwing techniques emphasize rapidity of execution and effectiveness when starting relatively far away, whereas Judo opponents, for example, are usually less than a meter away from each other. Although generally adapted for fighting at this distance, all Karate throwing techniques have their equivalent in Judo and Ju-Jitsu.

A **shoulder throw** involves throwing an opponent over the practitioner's shoulder. A shoulder throw which lifts the opponent from the ground is called a Back  Throw, while a throw which involves upsetting the opponents balance and pulling the opponent over the shoulder is referred to as Back Drop. Shoulder throws are one of the most used throws in Judo competition.

 In a **leg reap**, or sweep in some arts, the attacker uses one of their legs to reap one or both of their opponent's legs off the ground. Common leg reaps are Judo's *Ouchi Gari, Kouchi Gari, Osoto Gari,* and *Kosoto Gari,* there are similar techniques in wrestling. Generally, the opponent's weight is placed on the leg that is reaped away. This combined with the attacker's control of the opponent's upper body (with his/her hands) causes the opponent to fall over.

A **hip throw** involves
using the thrower's hip as a
pivot point, by placing the hip
in a lower position than an
opponent's center of gravity.
There are several basic types of
hip throws such as *O Goshi*. Hip throws in Judo are called *Koshi
Waza*, and in Aikido or Sumo they are called *Koshinage.*

Grappling and other

Grappling refers to techniques, maneuvers, and counters
applied to an opponent in order to gain a physical advantage,
such as improving relative position, escaping, submitting, or
injury to the opponent. Many martial arts styles use grappling
techniques to force submission of their opponent. It is also used
as counter techniques while adding a ground component to
their traditional martial arts training.

Some common grappling techniques are:

A **triangle choke** is a common choke
that is commonly used in wrestling. The
attacker wraps the neck of the opponent
with a V-shape form in the elbow or leg. The
attacker also squeezes their bicep/quad to
keep their opponent stabilize and effected.
Triangle chokes are primarily used in wrestling and Muay Thai.

Rolls are techniques that bring someone closer to their opponent, evade an attack, or advance quickly. Many martial arts such as Judo and Karate teaches the proper way to roll. During the roll, that individual should tuck their head and land on a shoulder for a smoother experience. Rolling also requires forward momentum to allow for faster and a more precise roll.

An **arm bar/lock** in grappling is a single or double joint lock that hyperextends the elbow joint and/or shoulder joint. An arm-lock that hyper flexes the shoulder joint is referred to as a shoulder lock, and an arm-lock that hyper extends the elbow joint is called an arm-bar. Obtaining an arm-lock requires effective use of full-body leverage in order to initiate and secure a lock on the targeted arm while preventing the opponent from escaping the lock.

A **neck crank** (neck lock) is a spinal lock applied to the cervical spine causing hyperextension either through bending, twisting, or elongating. A neck crank is typically applied by pulling or twisting the opponent's head beyond its normal ranges of rotation. Neck cranks are mainly banned from sports competitions due to its dangerous nature, but could be used as to defend oneself in a time of desperation.

Blocks

Blocking is the act of stopping or deflecting an opponent's attack by placing a limb across the line of the attack for the purpose of preventing injurious contact with the body. Styles and types of blocking, vary widely among the various martial arts. In Japanese martial arts, these techniques are referred to as *uke waza*. These include *age uke* (rising/high block) and *shuto uke* (knife hand block). In Korean martial arts, these techniques are referred to as *makgi*.

An **inside block** is an outward block that deflects a strike away from both attacker and  defender. To execute this, an inside forearm block would come from the hand on the same side of where the defender would want to push the strike. For example, if wanting to block a punch coming from the left, the defender would move his/her left hand outward to push the strike to the left as well, leaving the attacker open for a counter.

 An **outside block** is an inward block that deflects a strike away from the body. This block comes from a hand that comes inward (across the body) to deflect the strike leaving the defender slightly to the side of the strike causing it to miss. Typically, because of the

angles involved, an outside block are used against attacks aimed at the torso.

A **high block** deflects any downward strikes such as a hammer fist or a face punch from a taller opponent. The chamber starts low with the hand in a relaxed fist across the abdomen with the palm  facing inward. Then the hand travels from the inside of the body to above the defender's head at a 45-degree angle.

 A **low block** deflects an inward strike (such as a round kick) directed at the stomach, the ribs, or the common peroneal nerve. This block uses the outer forearm and has very similar mechanics to an inner block but lower.

References for part 1

1. Nevada, (1999) retrieved on September 22,2014 from http://boards.straightdope.com/sdmb/showthread.php?t=667009

2. Florence NG, (2014) retrieved on September 22,2014, from https://www.udemy.com/blog/best-martial-arts-for-self-defense/

3. Michelle, (2014), retrieved on September 2014, from http://www.urbandojo.com/blog/

4. Donn F. Draeger and P'ng Chye Khim (1979). Shaolin Lohan Kung-fu. Tuttle Publishing

5. http://beyondheroes2.altervista.org/martialartforms.htm

6. http://whichmartialarts.com/martial-arts-in-the-olympics/

7. https://en.wikipedia.org/
   a. J. R. Svinth (2002). A Chronological History of the Martial Arts and Combative Sports. Electronic Journals of Martial Arts and Sciences
   b. Zarrilli, Phillip B. A South Indian Martial Art and the Yoga and Ayurvedic Paradigms. University of Wisconsin–Madison
   c. Shahar, Meir (2000). "Epigraphy, Buddhist Historiography, and Fighting Monks: The Case of The Shaolin Monastery". Asia Major Third Series
      13

d. Thomas A. Green, Joseph R. Svinth (eds.), Martial Arts of the World: An Encyclopedia of History and Innovation, 2010, two volumes: vol. 1: 'Regions and Individual Arts', ISBN 9781598842449; vol. 2: 'Themes', ISBN 9781598842432

e. Kim, Wee-hyun. "Muyedobo T'ongji: Illustrated Survey of the Martial arts." Korea Journal 26:8 (August 1986): 42-54.

8. http://www.blackbeltwiki.com/

PART-2
MARTIAL SCIENCE

CHAPTER 4- PHYSICAL SCIENCE

4.1 Introduction

A close study of the traditional martial arts reveals an amazing use of sophisticated core principles of physical science. We have to admit that ancient science of scholars was more developed than what the world credits it to be. Harnessing and channeling the natural energy has been the basic principles of these martial arts. This is the reason why even a smaller human frame can knock down a much larger frame by using the understanding the principles of energy, force, intensity and momentum. In the section below, I look at the key principles of physics and analyze their usage in techniques.

4.2 Concepts of Physics

Force Mass acceleration 1st law

F=m*a	F=m*(change in velocity)/time

Martial Arts is a scientific system that varies the forces of the fight to your own advantage. Through the basic understanding of force by this formula we can change force in two ways:

Decreasing time increases acceleration which in turn increases the force given. The faster the mass is accelerated the more force is added. Both the greater the change in velocity and the decrease in amount of time taken increase acceleration.

Increasing mass is another viable way of increasing force. Martial artists maximize their force of impact by putting their whole body into the punch or kick. Each area of the body is moving at a different speed during a strike but at the same time. Using hips brings whole body forward at the same time. This aspect of kinetic linking is explained in a later physics chapter.

Overall, time must be small and mass must be high. It is much easier to force a small object to the same speed as the large object. From this logic we can see the smaller person will be able to accelerate faster with the same amount of force because his mass is less. This is where the smaller opponent has an advantage: speed. In later sections we will learn that speed is more important than mass when it comes to kinetic energy.

The fastest speed is at 80% of the length of the limb because the foot or fist must eventually decelerate to a velocity of zero. Therefore, the larger opponent will have a faster strike when the hand or foot reaches its target because of the greater distance and time allowed to accelerate. The larger opponent also has a greater mass which adds to the force.

Inertia 2nd law

m	$I=m*r^2$(varies)

Inertia is what makes objects difficult to move or difficult to stop moving. A bigger opponent will be harder to move away. Therefore, smaller opponent will be faster at moving if he/she is just as fit as the larger opponent.

When it comes to rotational inertia, a rotating object is harder to stop than a directly moving object. A normal object's inertia is just its mass (m) but a rotating inertia is $m*r^2$ and includes radius. A larger radius may come from longer length of spinning kicks. Though the greater the length of the kick the stronger it is, it also loses speed. Therefore, most kicks take more elliptical pathways because the knee and hip rotate at different times, like the round kick that does a final extension at the end of the kick with the knee. Moreover, rotation can even be added in every attack and block as seen later. Even strikes that follow a straight path have a rotation of the wrist, hip, ankle, torso, or shoulder.

In the real world other forces prevent movement outside the natural inertia, such as friction. Friction is the combination of gravity and the natural formation of the ground. Friction adds to the difficulty of moving the opponent. This is why the opponent takes damage rather than sliding away. The damage is what is converted into structural changes.

Equal and opposite reactions 3ʳᵈ law

When hitting something with a certain force the same force is always applied back to the person. Using this principle, blocks are just as effective at hurting the opponents. As another example, when hitting the ground, the ground hits back with the same amount of damage. The energy given back can be measure by the gravitational potential energy is *mgh*. Martial arts, therefore, may be based completely on blocking deflecting or takedown, even absent of any punches or kicking strikes

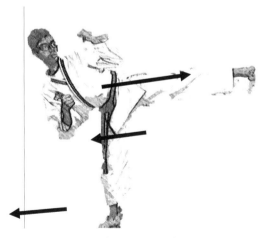

When punching an object, in order to stop itself from breaking the object must "hit" back with the same amount of

force. Sometimes however, the object cannot hit back because the force breaks through the object. The force continues as movement while the rest is translated into force in the object's movement and other forms of energy (we will see later). In the end, the person you punched now has broken bones and ruptured organs, or in a different case the board is splintered into pieces.

Rotational motion and Torque

$E = \frac{I\omega^2}{2} + \frac{mv^2}{2} + mgy^2$				
$I = mr^2$	$\tau = r \times F$	$\tau =$ torque	$r =$ length or radius of the arm lever	$F =$ magnitude of the force applied

Circular motion does not use the same laws of physics. As an effect of rotation, more energy is needed to stop a rotating object and more energy is needed to rotate the object (refer to section on inertia). When it comes to kicks, this additional force that has to be applied to overcome the mass of the foot is the torque, which is the tendency of a force to rotate an object about an axis or a fulcrum.

Torque is how the user makes sure the spin-kick *maintains* a spin. Power is the additional factor that makes spin-kicks so deadly. This is where the power equation comes in:

$$P = \frac{Fd}{t} \quad P = \tau^x \cdot \omega$$

The force needed to rotate an object also is added on by the shape of the object as well as the mass; therefore, a spinning strike with the same speed as a linear strike has much more power.

When it comes to punches adding twist to the punch can add extra damage. But in order to spin it the wrist must be properly aligned with the forearm. Therefore, doing a corkscrew motion when punching is likely to align the wrist and forearm horizontally, reducing injury while adding power.

Pressure

$$Pressure = \frac{F}{a}$$

The force of your attack spreads out across your palm and fingers. This dissipates the force of your attack over a fairly wide area. However, if you hold all of your fingers tightly together with only the side of your hands or only your finger tips that same amount of force is applied to a much smaller area. In that area the impact is much more focused making it more painful than using a palm heel strike. Sweeps use mass and gravity against opponent; the bigger they are the harder they fall. Falls work by spreading out the force over a larger area. As a result, spreading out arms at the point of impact during the fall reduces injury.

Most martial arts maximize the damage of force with pressure using the strongest parts of the body including elbows, knees, wrist, back of fist, two knuckles, ball of foot, heel, instep, spear hand, knife hand.

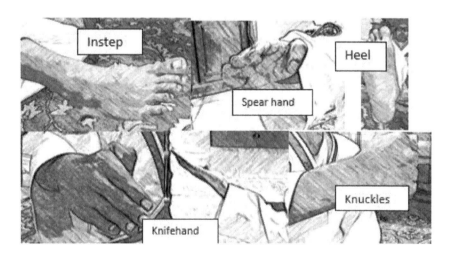

Center of mass

The key to maintaining a stable position is to maintain a stable center of gravity. Gravity pulls straight down towards the earth, so any off balancing moves makes martial artists susceptible to many moves, mainly throws and sweeps. Furthermore, the heavier your opponent, the larger the force of gravity that acts on him is. When a martial artist tries to unbalance his opponent he aims to rotate the body of the opponent around the opponent's center of mass. Gravity is the downward force which aids him in this. Because of gravity, in order to off-balance the opponent, all you must do is move his center-of-gravity outside its base. The gravity that acts on him at this point will make him lean or fall. Once he is there, he is off-balanced and all you have to do is pull him over a fulcrum (any body part including your own). Since he is in motion, he will stay in motion and fall over easily with little effort on your part to throw him.

In martial arts forms, you might pull opponents toward you to increase their forward momentum and throw them off balance. To protect against attacks, martial artists take on particular fighting stances. For example, generally, martial artists use a back stance with one leg in front of them and one leg behind them. This effectively shields the front of the body from attack like sweeps, and gives the Karateka better balance. Karateka hold themselves with their center of gravity relatively low to the ground, so it is more difficult for an opponent to knock them down. In different stances of different martial arts, the percentage of body weight should differ between legs back stance: 30% on front 70% on back. This kind of variation proves useful for preparing attacks quickly on the front leg as well as defense.

In a competition, martial artists concentrate on guarding themselves against attacks while waiting for an opening in their opponent's defenses. Using this defense, martial artists can focus on throwing attackers to the ground, which is a central, important element in other martial arts, notably Judo and Aikido.

Conservation of momentum and angles

$$p = \frac{L}{r}$$

When analyzing momentum in martial arts, assume two bodies of movement (the opponent and you) are interacting elastically, meaning all energy becomes kinetic energy from direct hits. Like any moving object, a punch or kick has its own **momentum**, the product of its mass and velocity. **Velocity** (and by extension, momentum) is not only a measurement of speed, but also of **direction**. To put it another way, two objects with equal mass and speed have a different momentum if they're going in different directions.

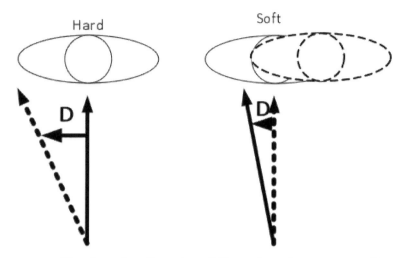

Hard and soft styles differ when it comes to linear and rotational momentum. Hard styles make more direct impact attacks, and in terms of momentum, hard styles deflect the opponent's momentum by blocking. When blocking, martial artists re-direct the hit controlling the direction of the attacker's momentum so that it goes at an angle. Since the strike is now on an angle, the defender feels much less force. In blocking, the objective is to intercept the strike so that it contacts your body from the side and redirects its momentum away from you. You do this by sweeping your opponent's arm or leg away from you with your own arm. Depending on the attack, martial artists may sweep a blow upward, downward or to either side. With this sort of blocking, you still end up colliding with your opponent, but you only feel a fraction of the force of the attack. As a metaphor, direction of momentum is at an angle to the wall. The momentum keeps the car moving forward, so the wall only feels a small fraction of the total force.

In contrast, soft styles redirect some of the momentum and use the energy against the person. In soft styles a natural rotation of direction is needed to reduce loss of energy. Soft styles allow the force not to be taken by the defender at all. The initial momentum of the attacker becomes the angular momentum of both the attacker and defender. And since the defender moves along with the attacker, the defender applies little to no torque at all. In the end, soft styles tend to use the motion of the attacker against him; basically, the opponent adds to his own destruction by adding to the momentum of the throw-down. Learning both strategies of hard and soft styles is the key to an all-around martial artist.

Impulse

Impulse (change in momentum) = force * time	Force = impulse / time

The amount of time a force is applied effects the change in momentum of the opponent. Therefore, a strike that is continuing to add force for a longer period of time or in other words keep going through the opponent will do much more damage rather than quick hit with *the same force*. Note the force must be continuous, or in other words continue speeding, which has limits due to limb length. It is this acceleration (change in momentum) that does the real damage in martial arts. This why a punch with more extension does more damage.

With impulse as a fixed quantity, force and time are necessarily inversely proportional. In other words, one can deliver a given amount of momentum by:

1. Transferring a large force for a short time; or

2. By transferring a smaller force over a longer time.

So, the longer it takes to transfer momentum, the less force is applied. If you want to maximize your force, you must ensure that as much of your momentum is transferred on impact as possible. This is true for both focused punches and follow-through punches used by boxers.

Impulse is related to power, but power is more applied in real world circumstances with friction and structural changes. This is because collisions in striking are inelastic meaning the kinetic energy is not conserved. The force of friction and structural compression is what converts the kinetic energy into damage.

Kinetic Linking

In the body, different parts are moving a different speeds relative to one another, but because they are moving together this leads to the concept of Kinetic linking; Kinetic linking is the

combination of two principals: Acceleration of distal segments by a proximal segment. In simpler terms, the movement of one segment tends to also move adjacent segments. This is because of the conservation of momentum. Momentum is always conserved in physics.

Kinetic linking is a more modern term for what ancient eastern martial arts have had for centuries. Other terms for it are Fa Jing or the Wave Form. The basic concept is that any attack is a whole body movement and power is not generated from the limb, but from the entire body. The way this is accomplished is to essentially "twist" your body along with your strike. Understanding that "twist" is an extremely simplistic way of describing what is essential to power in martial arts. The "kinetic link" is what takes weight classes out of fighting, it is what give the little guy stopping power against the big guy. You do not need to have huge muscles to do the wave form, you only need proper technique.

Imagine you center (or waist) as the fulcrum for your entire body. When you move to punch your center twists your body and the attacking side rotates forward while the opposite side rotates back, all simultaneously. Additionally, your posture throughout the movement must be anatomically natural: not leaning too forward, arms in line with shoulders, equally balanced. Furthermore, you must exhale out your mouth from the center (or your diaphragm) at the moment of impact. Finally, you must be loose through the movement, only tensing your muscles   at   the   moment   of   impact.

This attack movement can be done at any distance and is how power is generated for attacks like the one-inch punch.

Power

| $W=Fd$ | $P=W/t$ |

Work can be described as the amount of energy transferred by a force. In one case, a gloved cross punch, using the same force, transfers less energy to the opponent but uses the same amount of energy because the work (product of force and distance) is done on the gloves and the person. This is because the deformation of the glove gains changes the kinetic (moving energy) into potential energy. A smaller force may over a longer distance have the same damage as a large force over a small distance. Work thus gives the amount of energy or in this case damage imparted to the object.

The martial artist will usually more than compensate for any diffusion caused by gloves. He or she will do so by adding more "power". Power is how fast energy the same energy transferred. It is also the speed of the force. Power takes in account of time taken, so unlike doing work over a long period of time, a powerful attack gives no time to recover. Therefore, we can see which attack does the most destructive damage in a fight. Damage done in a shorter time is also more effective in taking down an opponent quickly. However, this also means that a great deal of training is concerned with power. In order to compensate for the diffusion of his/her force because of gloves, the martial artist has to work more in a shorter time.

Kinetic energy

Strikes are elastic, almost all kinetic energy made into deformation rather than the deflection. In mechanics, there are two types of energy, kinetic energy (moving) and potential energy (stored). $E=0.5mv^2+mgy$

What is happening when you begin to move into your strike is that the potential energy of your body is being translated to kinetic energy from the body. This kinetic energy in the body strike is then being transferred into potential energy for the strike the opponent rather than returning to the body.

Energy is not being created or destroyed, simply transferred from one state to another.

According to the kinetic energy formula ($0.5mv^2$) speed adds more energy than mass. Hence, speed is more important than mass, and a person will want to maximize speed in a strike. Remember, in a strike, the maximum speed in not at the end of the punch or kick but about 70% of the length of the striking distance.

Conserving Energy

The physics of martial arts are largely based on the concept of potential energy. The total amount of potential energy depends on the fighter's size muscle strength and physical health. And the object of Karate is to channel the energy of the body.

Generally, a stronger, larger person can exert more energy than a weaker, smaller person. But this doesn't necessarily determine the victor. Depending on the particular way you exert energy, you can vary the intensity and direction of the force you produce. A large force in a small time vs large time over a small force gives the same momentum and amount of energy.

Do not waste movement. If sparring, you usually need to conserve your energy. Remember to be quick, not fast. That is, move smoothly and without hesitation, instead of moving with jerks, or needing to move fast because you are out of position.

Keeping your body at the same height is also important for conserving energy. Every up-and-down movement by only 20 cm (7.8 inches) uses almost as much energy as a punch thrown at a speed of 7 m/s.

$$E=0.5mv^2+mgy$$

In nature, potential and kinetic energy is often symbolized with a spring. At rest, the spring has a great deal of potential, energy which is stored but not yet utilized. As the spring is set in motion, the potential energy changes to kinetic. Through its cycle, the energy is constantly cycling between potential energy at the stationary ends of the spring to kinetic. This ease and flow of energy within nature exemplifies the non-destructive properties of energy. Energy isn't simply created; it's transferred from one state to another. The greater the potential energy of an object, the greater the kinetic.

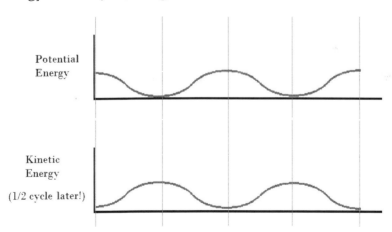

Because in the most simplistic terms, we equate movement with kinetic energy, the tendency is to utilize our potential strike energy within the movement of our body, not in the final impact. The most evident sign of this is the increase of tension within the arm or leg as one approaches the target. Tension is the transference of the potential energy of the strike back into the muscles of our body. Thus, if a Martial Artist can learn to remain relaxed and free of tension until the moment of the strike, they do not waste any energy and have the full pool of potential energy to strike with.

Breaking boards and people: Strain and breaking force

An average impact force is calculated and compared with that needed to break a human bone by stressing it beyond its ultimate bending stress value. Similar strain or breaking forces are needed to break bricks and wooden board.

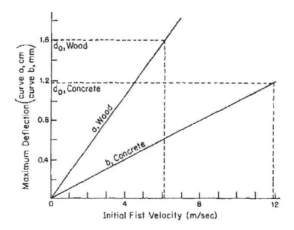

It is important that martial artists realize that results will vary from break to break due to factors such as the type of boards used and the striking point of the weight. Board quality often differs, so we purchase wood with few knots and cracks. In addition, the location on the board where the weight lands can affect whether or not the board will break. We get the best results by aiming for the middle of the board, because of the combination of the torque that allows the rotation of the two halves inwards. Momentum is continued when the boards are separated. Therefore, placing boards continuously without gap requires much more force to break a combine strain.

It has been determined that the palm strike is more effective than the punch for developing force and for transferring momentum, most likely the result of a reduced number of rigid links and joints. Also, a strike at head level is less effective than a strike at chest level for developing force and transferring momentum. This is because distance plays an effect on the overall force and momentum changes, and most likely is dependent on the velocity of the limb and alignment of the bones prior to impact.

Maximum hand velocity is actually achieved when the arm reaches 75-80% of extension. In other words the arm should still be bent. Since the hand cannot move forward a distance greater than the length of the arm, it must have a velocity of 0 at full arm's extension. To get the hardest hit, contact must be made with the object before this slowdown begins. Thus a good

Karate chop has a follow-through (as would a good tennis or golf swing). The hand is typically in contact with the object for fewer than five milliseconds.

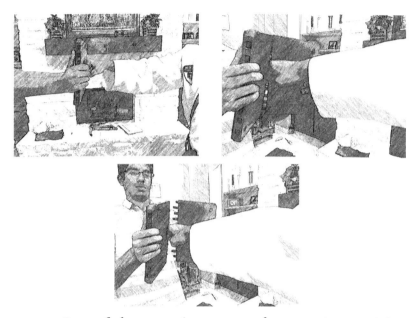

One of the most important elements in martial arts is **following through** on punches and kicks. When you hit something, say a piece of board, your natural instinct is to slow down your swing just before impact; you hesitate because you don't want to hurt your hand. Martial artists deprogram this **hesitation instinct**; they visualize pushing their fist to some point past their target (the other side of the board, for example).

The quicker the martial artist can make the strike, the larger the force transferred to the target. According to Newton's second law, the part of the object struck with this force will begin to accelerate or oscillate. Breakage occurs if the small area hit accelerates enough relative to the stationary ends of the object.

The object will experience strain and begin to crack from the bottom up.

4.3 Applied Physics

Kicks

The main parts of the kick: hip rotation, knee extension, foot position. The foot will have more momentum than punches due to longer length, do much greater about twice as much damage because of its mass and speed. In order to keep the foot in motion the user must apply torque. Using the full body momentum when in the air is also common in flying kicks

Faking kicks- Kicks like the tornadoes kick at first distract the opponent and lead up with an unexpected hit with full extension at the end, the built of speed of rotation is let out in the last second

Knee- accompanied with pulling the head down at the right angle, contact at the sternum, putting the hip into the hard sharp point of the knee cap adds power, concentrates the force by using pressure

Round kick- placement is key; uses quadriceps (the strongest muscle); the wider the distance from the body, the more the speed and power it picks; using the instep lowers surface area; increasing pressure; sometimes rapid succession of kicks is useful in first-getting the opponent off balance then leading with the power kick like the side kick

Side kick- leaning back slightly and bending the back knee allow the side kick to utilize the strongest muscle in the body, preparing for the kick by driving the knee up is also crucial, hip rotation

Heel/hook kick - rotating spinning hook/heel kicks come from the sudden spin of the front foot while evading or countering an attack, bring the foot back to the front

Front kick- snapping motion of the leg is like a released spring; the longer the rotation of the kick the greater the maximum speed it will reach; so in many cases, aiming higher is more effective with kicks

Kip-up- throws the weight of the legs to the bring the body's center of mass above ones feet

Crescent kick- uses different muscles than most kicks, your foot reaches max gravitational potential energy, the ease of downward acceleration creates max damage, also hard to see and coupled with surprise makes it most likely to hit

Punches

Punching gives much more control and direction.

Propelling the body in the air increases the impacting by using the body's full momentum

Bursting works completely different from hip rotation instead of converting rotational energy into the punch, the raw force of your legs hurling you forward

Eye poke/strike- the very low surface area the pressure is amplified onto, the soft tissues of the eyes, causes tremendous damage to it

Palm heel- Using the open hand involves almost no risk of injury to your hand. If you strike with your palm you cannot break your knuckles or fingers. Thus, it is relatively risk free. Almost any part of the head or neck can be an effective target and little training is necessary to use the palm strike. Using the palm heel however loses range. Since you are not using your bones (the hard knuckles), this is not as powerful as a normal punch.

Hammer fist- By using the momentum given by the shoulder through the whole body, the extension of the elbow brings a very fast and deadly rotational motion. Using your arms as a battering ram the hammer fist in rapid succession or in quick blow can be effective.

Elbow- Elbow strikes can be delivered in rapid speed in a small radius, which sacrifice distance for speed and strength pressure.

Reverse punch- The torso rotation adds 400% more power through kinetic links during this punch.

Knife hand strike- Because of the low surface area of the knife hand, if placed correctly on the vital parts of the neck, spinal damage will occur

Upper cut- Using the legs to push the arms up like a piston, this strike can severely damage the jaw and skull as well as the body only when bent over.

Blocks

Blocks defend against fatal attacks and also make room for your next one. It is the raw force of your legs hurling you forward. Deflecting the energy of the blow away from vulnerable parts. Harder blocks mean more deflection leaving him more open. Side steps are useful only for temporary escape.

The forearm is a very useful to block with. Using your field of vision, using your arms to defend different angles of attack, the deflection along the angle of your forearm reduces the impact. Forearm blocks also include the rotation of the elbow to move the attacker out of the way.

During a choke the opponent is relying on his grip strength and outstretched arms to maintain the choke; an easy solution is to use your back and shoulder muscles, which are much stronger, to break free.

Blocking guns; pulling the attacker forwards causes him to lose balance and at the same time loosen his wrist to prepare for a fall (or break his hand). The barrel of the gun then becomes a lever.

Joint Locking/Chokes

Joint Locks- The usage of levers that damage the joints using high toque pinch points -the greater the torque the greater the pain.

Neck crank- Joint locking of the neck is allowed by using the arm, while holding the other persons arm behind him like a lever and putting your elbow on his neck.

Arm lock- With the elbow locked, the elbow becomes a fulcrum and the forearm becomes the lever, the mechanical advantage of leverage doubles any force done, all by using the opponents own arm.

Knee bar- locks the opponent's knee and you use your hips as the fulcrum, this can destroy even the strongest ligaments of the knee

Arm bar- legs push up on opponents neck your arms apply downward pressure on his trapped wrist, elbow become a fulcrum point

Leg ankle lock (*ashi hishigi*) - The torque of this lock allows it to even break the tibia and fibula – the strongest bones in the body.

Chokes- Blocking arteries in the neck using biceps or legs, constricting blood flow from the carotid arteries to the brain

Triangle choke- putting the opponent's neck and arm between one of you straight legs and the other bended leg

Throws/Sweep

Throws and sweeps both affect the conditional stability lifting the person off the ground, disturb center of mass and make resistance impossible.

Use of leverage and Center of mass- during a throw down the center of mass must be over the center

These use the force of gravity added with kinetic + gravitational potential.

Hip throw (*uchi mata*) - thrusting your hips into the opponents waist creates a pivot point. The throw is like a crowbar using the hip as the fulcrum and leg as the lever.

Kata-gatame- To assure your opponent is trapped you must keep your center of gravity below his, grabbing around his neck locking your other arm on the other side all while pushing down using your body weight keeping your hips below his next to him.

Ippon seoi nage- Where the arm is the lever where your shoulder is the pivot, while you bend over, the opponent is thrown over your back.

Osoto otoshi- Pushing the opponent above the center of mass, while using the leg to trip the opponent under his center of mass makes an easy knock down

Falls and rolls

Breaking fall are necessary, to preventing injury to the whole body. In the front fall, slapping the front of the palm while falling with a bended arm is a technique that minimizes the damage done by gravitational energy by spreading it out the body. It also redirects the damage away from the head, which could have caused unconsciousness as well as bruising. When falling back, the natural roll of the spine while the arms extend and slap the ground behind.

Rolls decrease force of an impact on the ground: less time on ground causes less damage, more area dispersed relieves pressure, and momentum of the body caused by gravity is transferred into rotational momentum. Side rolls use the shoulder to the hip to roll rather than the spine, reducing the chance of damage.

Weapons

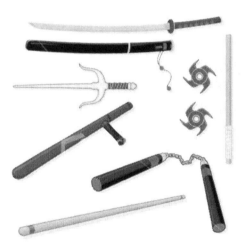

Weapons in martial arts are no more than an extension of the body. In fact, some weaponless martial arts were developed from the use of weapons. By following the laws of physics, the extra distance gives a powerful advantage even beyond reach. For one thing, with just the flick of the wrist the tip of the weapon is moving many times faster. Fear of damage done to the one's own body when attacking is also removed.

Safety gear

In the United States, approximately 1.5 million to 2 million persons practice the martial arts. Martial arts is generally safer than other contact sports because of low incentive to cause injury. This is because martial artists gravitate the martial arts towards self-defense, improve cardiovascular fitness, flexibility, and self-esteem. Some join for the structured exercise programs, whereas others desire the artistic expression or have the need to compete.

Injuries involve the head and neck region, trunk, and extremities. Soft tissue trauma, hematomas, and lacerations are some of the most common injuries. Occasionally fractures occur, most often involving the hands and digits. The neurosurgical literature indicates that wearing headgear increases the shearing injury to nerve fibers and neurons in the brain in proportion to the degree of acceleration to the head. Three case presentations illustrate death resulting from anterior chest trauma.

A 5-year national survey of martial arts was done using the National Electronic Injury Surveillance System (NEISS).

Seventy-four percent of the injuries involved the extremities and 95% were mild to moderate in nature. Even though most of the injury types were contusions/abrasions (36%), lacerations (14%), and sprains/strains (28%), 15% were dislocations and fractures. Five percent of all injuries were severe, and there were 18 hospitalizations. There were no deaths. Weapon-related injuries were rare and never serious. Overall, the risk of serious injury in the sport was found to be low, especially when compared to other contact sports.

Essential tips:

- Headgear is essential when sparring.
- Cups and protective waist belts add protection to the groin area.
- Use a mouth guard to protect your teeth, mouth, and tongue.
- If you wear glasses, use safety glasses or glass guards to protect your eyes.
- Wrap your hands with the appropriate sized wraps and with proper technique. Properly wrapped hands will feel secure.
- Proper footwear is important. On matted floors, avoid socks or footwear that may cause you to slip. In many cases, going barefoot provides the most stability. Talk to your coach or supervisor about what type of footwear would be best for your activity and skill level.
- Being thrown by an opponent at high speed, or falling onto one's neck or head, can result in serious injury.

- New techniques should be practiced at half speed. It is also helpful to talk to your coach or supervisor before attempting a new move to ensure you understand how to safely execute it.
- Know how much force may inflict injury.
- Know your opponent's level of experience. Newer participants may not understand when they are in danger of injury.
- Practice in a well-padded area.
- Be aware of your surroundings while other participants are practicing to avoid collisions.
- In case of a joint problem, the participant must have no pain, no swelling, full range of motion, and normal strength.
- In case of concussion, the participant must have no symptoms at rest or with exercise, and should be cleared by a qualified medical professional.

CHAPTER 5- BIOLOGY – SCIENCE OF DEFENSE IN MARTIAL ARTS

5.1 Introduction:

While Physics in martial arts primarily helps us understand the mechanics of offense, Biology, on the other hand, sheds light on exploiting or harnessing the strength and weakness of human body. Good understanding of human anatomy is vital to maximize potential of attack as well as defense against one. Understanding facts and science about our bones, muscles, joints, cartilage, ligaments and tendons is of utmost importance to master the art kicks, punches, chokes, strikes ...etc.

To excel in martial arts one requires endurance, flexibility, reaction time and agility. All these skills require a very good physical conditioning on all key human anatomy.

Every martial artist must understand the anatomy of human body to reflect the strength and weakness. This is key to protection during aggression or defense.

5.2 Human Anatomy: Bones

Bones are key targets in self-defense and also used as a key tool for attacking opponents. There are about 206 bones in an adult human body. Bones grow in humans until in 20's and achieve maximum density at around age 30. The human skeletal system has six major functions including the production of blood cells, for support, for movement, for protection, for storage of ions and endocrine regulation.

Bones if broken will re-grow and repair themselves. Like our skin or muscles, the human body's bones are also constantly worn down and re-made. It is commonly acknowledged that every 7 years we essentially have a new bone.

The majority of human bones have a dense, strong outer layer, followed by a spongy part full of air for lightness, while the middle contains a soft, flexible, tissue substance called bone marrow. Bone marrow makes up 4% of a human body mass. It produces red blood cells which carry oxygen all over the body. Marrow also produces lymphocytes, key components of the lymphatic system, which support the body's immune system. Calcium is very important for our bones and helps keep them strong and healthy.

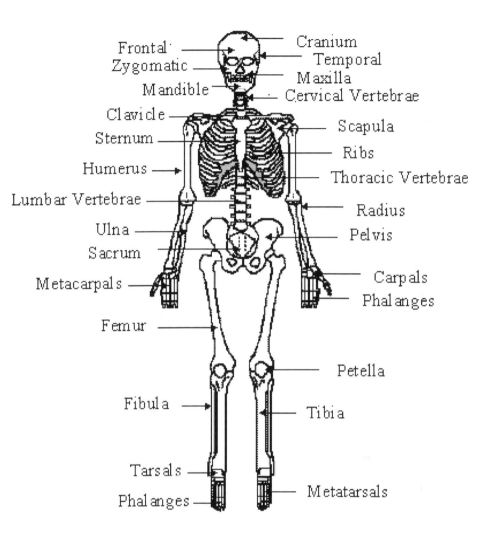

Frontal
Zygomatic
Mandible
Clavicle
Sternum
Humerus
Lumbar Vertebrae
Ulna
Sacrum
Metacarpals
Femur
Fibula
Tarsals
Phalanges

Cranium
Temporal
Maxilla
Cervical Vertebrae
Scapula
Ribs
Thoracic Vertebrae
Radius
Pelvis
Carpals
Phalanges
Petella
Tibia
Metatarsals

Head & Neck Area:

The bones of the head and neck play the vital role of supporting the brain, sensory organs, nerves, and blood vessels in the head and protecting these structures from mechanical damage. The skull consists of 22 cranial and facial bones, which, encases and protects the brain as well as the special sense organs such as vision, hearing, balance, taste, and smell.

Striking at the head and neck area is common in martial arts. Although counted as prize hits for fighters, it could also be potentially very damaging for the opponent such as unconsciousness. Techniques such as knife hands, head-butts and other strikes aimed at the head score the most points as well as increase damage and give mental advantage to attacker.

To understand this, we will look at some key bones in the head and neck area and evaluate the vulnerability of these bones.

Cranium (skull) - as a whole is comprised of multiple bones (8) stitched together to form the brain case:

- **Frontal bone (Forehead)** - The frontal bone is a bone of the skull found in the forehead region. The frontal bone plays a vital role in supporting and protecting the delicate nervous tissue of the brain. It gives shape to the skull and supports several muscles of the head. The center of this bone (often near the hairline) is the hardest portion and can be used in the forward head-butt.

- **Temporal Bone** - The temporal bone is one of two bones that form parts of the sides and base of the cranium. It's a common target for a knockout strike since it is located next to the temporal lobes in the cerebral cortex.

- **Zygomatic bone**- The zygomatic bone is one of two bones (sometimes called malar bones) that are responsible for the prominences of the cheeks below and to the sides of the eyes. They form part of the eye socket, so any strike in the area (a solid palm heel strike or a regular punch) can cause internal bleeding of the socket.

- **Maxilla & Mandible (Jaw Bone)** - The maxilla consists of maxillary bones that form the upper jaw; together they are the keystone of the face, for all other immovable facial bones are connected to them. It's a common target for punches and elbow strike. Striking this location can break the jaw, dislocate the "hinge", and even cause multiple fractures to bone structures by the ear

- **Cervical bones**- Consists of 7 bones that make up the neck portion of the spine (there are 7 of them). Cervical vertebrae are the thinnest and most delicate vertebrae in the spine but offer great flexibility to the neck. They encase the spinal cord but due to their smaller size can be fractured and cause nerve damage. A typical "Karate chop" can inflict damage to these bones.

Upper Trunk – Shoulder & Arm:

- **Clavicle (Collar bone)** - The clavicle is a pair of long bones that connect the scapula to the sternum. The clavicle is one of the most commonly broken bones in the human body.

Knife hands or elbow strikes (even an axe kick) are common techniques to hit this area.

- **Scapula (Shoulder blade)** - It anchors the humerus to the clavicle. Over dozen muscles are attached to this. Although it is hard to reach, fracturing it with an elbow strike would impair its function.

- **Sternum**- The sternum, commonly known as the breastbone, is a long, narrow flat bone that serves as the keystone of the rib cage and stabilizes the thoracic skeleton. Several muscles that move the arms, head, and neck have their origins on the sternum. It also protects several vital organs of the chest, such as the heart.

- **Humerus (Upper arm bone)** - The humerus is the both the largest bone in the arm and the only bone in the upper arm. Many powerful muscles (biceps & triceps) that manipulate the upper arm at the shoulder and the forearm at the elbow are anchored to the humerus. Commonly used for bar or blocks.

- **Radius (Inside forearm bone)** - The radius is the more lateral and slightly shorter of the two forearm bones and is found along the inside of the thumb. It is found on the thumb side of the forearm and rotates to allow the hand to pivot at the wrist. Used for a block that implements blocking/striking at the inside of the arm. These movements are also essential to many everyday tasks such as writing, drawing, and throwing a ball.

- **Ulna (Outside forearm bone)** - This is a fairly strong bone as it is the main force behind blocking (with the arm) in martial arts though commonly broken by a fall. The ulna is the longer, larger and more medial of the lower arm bones. Many muscles in the arm and forearm attach to the ulna to perform movements of the arm, hand and wrist. Movement of the ulna is essential to such everyday functions as throwing a ball and driving a car.
- **Ribs**- The true ribs are attached to the sternum (breastbone) directly by their costal cartilages. There are seven true ribs. (The other ribs are termed floating or false ribs.)
- **Thoracic vertebrae**- The 12 vertebrae in the chest region form the spine's thoracic region. Thoracic vertebrae are larger and stronger than cervical vertebrae but are much less flexible.

Hand & Wrist:

- **Carpals (Wrist bones)** - There are 8 of these little bones that facilitate in the movement of the hand. They can be broken during an unprotected fall or with enough pressure to the back of the hand (in wrist lock) which could cripple the hand.
- **Metacarpals (Hand bones)** - These five bones are between the fingers and carpals making up the hand. The

heads of the metacarpal bones form the knuckles a key asset during fights.

- **Phalanges (Fingers)** - Small bones that make up the skeleton of the fingers and thumb. Apart from grabbing it can be used to targets eyes or throat.

Lower trunk- Hips & Legs:

- **Lumbar vertebrae (Lower back bones)**- The 5 vertebrae in the lower back form the lumbar region of the spine These are the largest and strongest of the vertebrae as they support the central mass of your body weight. A knee strike to this area would be painful.
- **Pelvis**- Located in the lower torso, the pelvis is a sturdy ring of bones that protects the delicate organs of the abdominopelvic cavity while anchoring the powerful muscles of the hip, thigh, and abdomen

Lower extremity - Leg:

- **Femur (Thigh bone)** - The femur is the longest, heaviest, and strongest bone in the entire human body. All of the body's weight is supported by the femurs during many activities, such as running, jumping, walking, and standing. A strong scoop or shin kick could break the bone at this point (aimed at the top of the thigh) and result in the common broken "hip".

- **Tibia (Shin)** - is the larger and stronger of the two lower leg bones. It forms the knee joint with the femur and the ankle joint with the fibula and tarsus. Many powerful muscles that move the foot and lower leg are anchored to the tibia. Used a lot in Muay Thai shin kicks.

- **Patella (Knee Cap)** - the triangular-shaped bone at the front of the knee joint, it protects the knee joint. This is a fairly strong bone/mechanism for striking with but a direct hit to patella could fracture it and impair the muscular movement of the lower leg.

- **Fibula (Calf bone)** - The fibula is the long, thin and lateral bone of the lower leg. Because this bone runs on the lateral (outside) side of the leg it can be fairly easily broken from a fall or a shin kick, resulting in a typical "broken ankle".

- **Tarsal** - The seven bones that make up the ankle. They form a durable complex but can be fractured from rolling the ankle more severely than a sprain

- **Metatarsals**- The metatarsal bones are five long, cylindrical bones in the foot. The ends of these bones make the ball of the foot which is the striking surface of a basic front kick. Impact from a heel kick could easily break/fracture these bones quickly hindering the function of the foot.

- **Phalanges (Toes)** - They are fragile, for example needing to be curled forward during a groin kick or pulled back during a basic front kick. Breaking/fracturing them with a keel kick is painful, movement hindering, and allows for a quick get away from an attacker

5.3 Human Anatomy: Muscle

The muscular system is an organ system in which bones of the skeleton are combined and merged with muscles and tendons in order that your body can move. Besides moving it can make up the posture and circulate your blood throughout the whole body. There are several parts in the muscular system, especially in muscles, in both anterior and posterior. The following diagrams are the example of muscular system.

While most people associate muscles with strength, they do more than assist in lifting heavy objects. The 650 muscles in the body not only support movement, they also help to maintain posture and circulate blood and other substances throughout the body, among other functions.

Key muscles in human body are explained in this section.

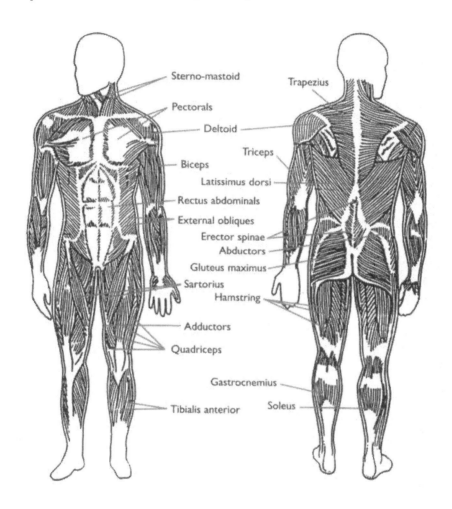

Classification of Muscles:

Types of Muscles

The muscular system can be broken down into three types of muscles: skeletal, smooth and cardiac.

Skeletal muscles are the only voluntary muscle tissue in the human body and control every action that a person consciously performs. Most skeletal muscles are attached to two bones across a joint.

Smooth, muscle is found inside organs such as the stomach and intestines, as well as in blood vessels.

Cardiac muscle (found in the heart) is an involuntary muscle responsible for pumping blood throughout the body.

Muscle shapes

Muscles are further classified by their shape, size and direction. The deltoids, or shoulder muscles, have a triangular shape.

Size can be used to differentiate similar muscles in the same region. The gluteal region (the buttocks) contains three muscles differentiated by size: the gluteus maximus (large), gluteus medius (medium) and gluteus minimus (smallest), the NIH noted.

The direction in which the muscle fibers run can be used to identify a muscle. In the abdominal region, there are several sets of wide, flat muscles

Muscles also can be identified by their function. The flexor group of the forearm flexes the wrist and the fingers. The supinator is a muscle that allows you to roll your wrist over to face palm up.

Depending on what you feel your style needs, it is up to you to decide whether to focus on more power, or hand speed, endurance, or all of it.

The key to effective boxing training is understanding how your muscles are used in boxing and to be able to decide how to train them to best fit that purpose. Smart athletes will know that certain muscles should definitely be given priority over the others.

Arms:

Arms deliver power an important function is to connect the power to the opponent. It's worth noting that arm is not responsible for generating power, it's the leg which is the primary generator. All your arms need to do is to connect the power generated by your body to your opponent.

Arms are meant for connecting punches, it's more important to have fast arms than powerful arms. Fast arms give you that speed and snap. The speed helps you sneak that punch past your opponent's defense. The snap helps you recover that arm quickly to defend yourself after punching.

Key muscled in arms are:

- The **Bicep** is the muscle that sits on the front of the upper arm. The biceps are for the speed and snap of your hooks and uppercuts. The typical bicep curl with weights is a great exercise as well as a standard variety of pushups. A quick strike to this muscle can surprisingly be helpful in controlling or blocking an attack.

- The **Tricep** is on the back of the upper arm. This is actually the muscle that helps deliver the force of strikes (speed) as its purpose is to extend the arm outwards. Pushups are a great way to strengthen this muscle

Bulking up your arms for power is not recommended, keep them lean and fast allows for fast punches and fast combinations in. The muscles of the arm and hand are specifically designed to meet the body's diverse needs of strength, speed, and precision while completing many complex daily tasks.

Small Muscles

The neck is for punch resistance. You'll see many fighters strengthening their neck so that their head doesn't get whip-lashed and left in a more vulnerable angled position when it gets hit by punches. The forearm muscles are for tightening your fist harder when you punch. A tighter fist means your hand will hit with a more solid punch. At the same time, a tighter fist means your hand is less likely to be injured since the bones don't have much room to move around and get misaligned.

- The **Sternocleidomastoid** helps the head rotate to the side and pull the head down. Useful in looking around to your surroundings and pulling the head down for a head-butt. The neck as a whole should be stretched in all directions as some people harbor a lot of tension/stress in their neck when doing high impact activities.

Frontal and Upper Body Core- Chest & Abs

The chest muscles are your upper body core muscles. Its most important functions is to connect the shoulders, arms, and latissimus dorsi (lats) into one combined force. They also generate the most punching power out of your upper body muscles.

Abs (Frontal Body Core & Snap)

The abdominal muscles are a very powerful set of muscles that hold the whole body together. Our abs allow you to connect the force generated by all your limbs into one powerful punch. Aside from connecting your whole body together the abdominal muscles help you breathe and allow you to take frontal body shots.

Key muscles group

- The **Pectoralis** muscle is the breast muscle of the chest. Primary function is to pull the arms inwards, it improves the power of arm strikes and can act to dampen internal trauma from strikes to the chest.

- The **Rectus/Transverse Abdominis (Six pack)** are the superficial and deep muscles of the stomach ("Abs"). Apart from aesthetic purposes it can help one absorb punch to the gut with little damage. This can be accomplished through slight toning of the abs and proper training. Best exercises for this includes planks and v-sits.

- The **Serratus** and **Obliques** are the muscles on the upper and lower sides of the body. They cover the ribs and the gap between the lower ribs and the hips. Often worked out for aesthetics but provide very good reinforcement of ribs and the sides of the trunk. This helps the body better withstand impact such as punches or kicks.

Hips and Back (Lower Body Core & Rear Body Core)

The hips hold your lower body and legs together. They also generate a huge amount of power by pivoting your whole body when you need. Another important function is that your hips have to do with how well you are balanced. Since your hips are very close to your body's center-of-gravity, stronger hips would mean that you have better control of your balance.

The back also functions as a total body core muscle by holding the body together and combining the power generated by all your limbs. Although little known but commonly believed that back helps a lot in punch recovery i.e. the speed of how fast you can pull your hand back after a punch. That is why it's recommended not to neglect workout to condition back.

Key muscles area in this area are

- The **Trapezius** is a triangular going from the back of the neck, to the shoulder blade, and to the spine around the center of the back. This muscle helps stabilize the scapula and the neck. Working this muscle will improve posture, preventing a sore neck from intense workouts, and condition it to the impact of rolls.

- The **Latissimus dorsi** is a large broad muscle that stretches from the mid/lower back to the humerus of the arm. Its function is prevalent in nearly every arm movement and because of its function and position is important to martial artists channeling energy up through the hip to the arm for a strike. This muscle is most improved by exercises such as pull-ups, rowing, and dead lifting.

- The **Glutes** (there are three of them being the maximus, medius, and minimus) that run from the pelvis to the head of the thigh joint. They assist in keeping the body upright, and most powerful function is pulling the body upright from being bent over. These muscles can be worked through heavy cardio or exercises such as squats, hips thrusts, and more. To the martial artist they can aid in regaining balance after kicks and in the transfer of energy in upward strikes such as an uppercut or rising elbow.

Legs

Legs is the biggest muscles in or body, not only it generates the most power by pushing off the ground but also instrumental in pivoting and rotating. Key muscles are the quads and the calf muscles.

- The **Quadriceps (Quads)** are the muscles found on the top of the thigh and function together mostly to pull the upper leg closer to the body and extend the lower leg. These muscles help put a lot of forward power into kicks and can also be a good target for shin kicks to an opponent.

- The **Hamstrings** is another large group of muscles, located on the back of the thigh, the help pull the upper and lower leg back. This is another important group to stretch for better flexibility and height of kicks, as well as pulling the leg back quicker from a kick to avoid an opponent grabbing your kick. Running is a great and easy way to improve the power of these muscles, while to touches and leg lifts are a great way to stretch the muscles.

- The **Calf** is a collection of muscles on the back of the lower leg mostly made up of the **Gastrocnemius** which work to make the foot move up and down, moderately useful to most kicks, but is worked out in most moderately strenuous activities.

5.4 Human Anatomy: Joints

Joints are the place where two bones meet or connect. Each joint is specialized in its shape and structure to control the range of motion between the parts that it connects. Joints differ in their normal range of motion, relative strength and usefulness.

Joints may be classified functionally based upon how much movement they allow.

Fixed joints -Fixed joints, are fixed and don't allow any movement. A joint that permits no movement is known as a synarthrosis. The bones in the skull are held together with fibrous connective tissue. These joints are made of tough collagen fibers. Skull is a good example of this joint.

Slightly movable joints -These joints are found in intervertebral disks of the spine and in the hips, they have a slight amount of movement at the joint. They are also called cartilaginous joints and are made of a band of cartilage that binds bones together. Examples of cartilaginous joints include joints between the ribs and costal cartilage, and the intervertebral disks of the spine.

Synovial joints - They are movable joints featuring a fluid-filled space between smooth cartilage pads at the end of articulating bones containing a lubricating liquid called synovial fluid. There are many different types of synovial joints in the body, such as gliding, hinge, saddle, and ball and socket joints.

Ball & Socket Joint:

Ball and socket joints, like the one found in our hip and shoulder joints, are the most mobile type of joint in the human body. They allow you to swing your arms and legs in many different directions. These joints have the freest range of motion of any joint in the body – they are the only joints that can move in a full circle and rotate around their axis. However, the drawback to the ball and socket joint is that its free range of motion makes it more susceptible to dislocation than less mobile joints.

The *hip joint* is a very important ball-and-socket synovial joint. Functionally, the hip joint enjoys a very high range of motion. The ball-and-socket structure of the joint allows the femur to move freely through a 360-degree circle. The femur may also rotate around its axis about 90 degrees at the hip joint. Only the *shoulder joint* provides as high of a level of mobility as the hip joint

Gliding Joint:

Gliding joints occur between the surfaces of two flat bones that are held together by ligaments which allows for the bones to glide past one another in any direction. Some of the bones in our wrists and ankles move by gliding against each other. Gliding joints are also formed in the axial skeleton throughout the neck and trunk to improve the flexibility of these regions.

Hinge Joint

A hinge joint is a common class of synovial joint that includes the ankle, elbow, and knee joints. Hinge joints are formed between two or more bones where the bones can only move along one axis to flex or extend. Hinge joints, such as the elbow and knee, limit movement in only one direction so that the angle between bones can increase or decrease at the joint. The limited motion (allows up to 180 degrees of movement) at hinge joints provides for more strength and reinforcement from the bones, muscles, and ligaments that make up the joint.

Due to its limited unidirectional movement, putting pressure can snap these joints.

Saddle Joint

A saddle joint is a synovial joint where one of the bones forming the joint is shaped like a saddle with the other bone resting on it like a rider on a horse

Saddle joints, such as the one between the first metacarpal and trapezium bone, permit 360-degree motion by allowing the bones to pivot along two axes. Our thumb is an example of saddle joint.

5.5 Human anatomy: Ligament & Tendon

Ligaments and tendons are like the support cables that connect bone to bone and muscle to bone, allowing your body to move where you want when you want while keeping everything aligned in the right way. Every muscle has a tendon, every joint has at least one ligament.

Tendons

The key function of the tendon is to connect muscle tissue to bone. For example, our Achilles' tendon attaches muscles to our heel. Tendons are thicker and stronger than muscles; they can handle the force of several muscles simultaneously to perform the movements necessary. Unlike muscles, tendons only come in one type of fiber.

Ligaments

Ligaments strictly connect bones to other bones (not muscles), allowing the joint to maintain connection and provide support, control and stability in many different ways and directions. Hinge joints (elbow, knee), or ball & socket joints like your shoulders or hips are dynamic and require much more support to tie up the joints.

For example, one of the most common and prone to injury is the knee joint ligaments, knee joint is supported by four different ligaments. The MCL- medial collateral ligament, connects the thigh bone (femur) from above to the shin (tibia) bone below it on the inside of your knee and limits sideward movement of your knee. Its counterpart, the LCL -lateral collateral ligament (LCL), also connects the femur to the tibia, this time on the outside of your knee, limiting its movement sideways.

Inside the knee are two ligaments that limit movement of the femur and tibia forwards and backwards. The anterior cruciate ligament (ACL) connects the femur and tibia through the center of your knee and prevents the tibia from moving too far forward or rotating too far inwards or outwards. The other ligament that runs through the middle of your knee is the posterior cruciate ligament (PCL), and prevents your tibia from moving too far back of your femur.

5.6 Human anatomy – Cartilage

Cartilage is a fibrous and rubbery connective tissue found throughout the vertebrate skeletal system. As with other connective tissues, the general function of cartilage is to support and connect different parts of the body. Cartilage is made up of specialized cartilage cells called chondrocytes. Cartilage is softer, more compressible, and more elastic than bone. Adults have cartilage in joints, in the nose, ears, breastbone, trachea, and larynx, and at the ends of bones.

Cartilage also helps to reduce friction between the bony elements of a joint. A lubricating liquid called synovial fluid helps the cartilage-covered bones of the shoulder slide over each other more easily. Cartilage found in joints with a large range of motion is called smooth cartilage. In joints that experience more limited motion, cartilage plays a different role. In this kind of joint, the cartilage that holds the bones together is called elastic cartilage. Immovable joints are held together by fibrous cartilage.

Cartilage is very important tissue of the body. Cartilage damage is very serious and therefore important to prevent as well as know the tactical use of damaging cartilage during self-defense situations.

Nose

There are several pieces of cartilage that make up the nose, the most notable of which being the septal cartilage that forms the central sturdy part of the nose between the two nostrils. This is the major portion of cartilage that will break often during fight (hook/straight punch, head but, palm/elbow strike) causing bleeding to occur, usual a snapped nose heals within couple weeks.

Ear

The external portion of the ear covered in skin is made up of a one-piece cartilage called the auricle. During defense a strong enough pull can rip the ear from the side of the head and cause a lot of bleeding.

Chest

This is the cartilage that directly links the ribs in the front of the chest to the sternum. This allows for the chest to comfortably expand and recoil after moderate impact. With the true ribs these are short segments of cartilage while at the false ribs they are longer segments that have to ascend and merge with others to be able to attach to the sternum. This is sturdy cartilage but can be damaged under high impact like a knee strike.

5.7 Biology of Punches and Strikes

Punches and strikes are most commonly used offensive technique in martial arts.

Although punches can be thrown anywhere at the body, hitting on the face is most prized. A human's protruding jaw, thick brow ridge above the eyes, robust bones around the nose and upper jaw and large molars and premolars are defining characteristics designed to absorb hits but the power and angle can still inflict severe injury.

Punch to Chest- Knocking the wind out

Punch to the chest lead to the symptom commonly called "getting the wind knocked out of you".

Many fighters and martial artists experiences a difficulty of breathing upon receiving a strike to the chest. This is due to the pressure on Solar Plexus, a complex network of nerves located in the abdomen, at the end of the sternum, which then results in spasm of diaphragm, an organ located under the lungs that raises and lowers to either fill the lungs with, or expel them, of air. When the diaphragm spasms, although the lungs are still able to contract and expand to allow the fighter to breathe, the spasm in combination with the pain as a result of the strike make it difficult for the lungs to fill with air, resulting in a momentary difficulty of breathing for the fighter. Although one recovers after a rest, we must watch for any other symptoms.

Punch to the Ear (Cauliflower ear)

In a self-defense situation, a jab, hook punch or straight punch can be thrown at the ear. Although these strikes are usually intended for the temple to for a "knock out" punch but will often misses and land on the zygomatic arch or can hit the ear causing damage. A clean hit can disrupt an assault or disorient an attacker. Allowing time to recompose. A hit can cause physical damage, ripping to the ear, primarily a cartilage. With time it heals. A hard direct hit can also lead to dislocation of ossicular chain transferring the kinetic energy into the skull. This can result in about 60 dB of hearing loss.

Strikes at nose:

Strikes such as hook punch, head-butt, palm and elbow strike can shatter or likely to snap the nose cartilage. There are several pieces of cartilage that make up the nose, the most notable of which being the septal cartilage that forms the central sturdy part of the nose between the two nostrils. This is the major portion of cartilage that will break often causing bleeding to occur. A typical/simple broken nose where the septum is snapped to one side or the other will take 1-2 weeks to heal.

5.8. Biology of Choke

Chokes - some of which focus on the windpipe while others focus on the arteries stopping blood flow to the brain

The trachea (windpipe), is a lengthy tube of muscle and cartilage that is used for passage of air from outside into the lungs. The cartilage holds the pipe open to allow for a steady passage of air, and the mucus lining aids in filtering the air passing into the lung by trapping particles. Although the trachea is essential in human breathing for humans, it's very exposed and susceptible to damage. It takes about 8olb of pressure, equal to crumple an empty can of soda, to crush the trachea. Upon collapsing, smaller blood vessels begin to seep in the lungs, the diameter shrinks combined with pain, and breathing becomes difficult. The volume of air that can be used by the body declines due to the displacement caused by the blood. Because of the obvious applicability of trachea weaker design, it makes a valuable target for the defender fighter.

5.9 Biology of Kick

Any martial art using kicks can produce serious trauma. The fact that the leg generates enormous power means the use of it can be lethal.

Kick at Neck:

Kick at neck area, if not blocked can incapacitate the opponent. Located in the neck, adjacent to the carotid artery and Pneumogastric nerve (controls sensory, motor and secretory function of vital organs including heart). As known, nerves communicate information such as pain through sodium channels. Under the circumstances that the nerve is struck with a force, nerve cells would immediately respond by flaring sodium through the channels rapidly, sending the signal of intense pain to the brain at speeds nearly undetectable to by the defender fighter. The brain then responds using those same sodium channels, shutting down several vital organs and slowing the heart down significantly to a dangerous rate, resulting in asphyxiation of the body. Kung-Fu includes a palm-heel strike to the left side of the chest, a direct strike to the heart can shut the heart. Tae-kwon-do side kick can also be applied to the left ribcage, where significant force may cause heart contractions.

5.10 Biology of Joint Locks/ Manipulations:

Joint manipulation in the martial arts is used to control a subject, take them to the ground, or immobilize the affected limb.

Joint locks manipulate wrists, elbows, knees, etc., beyond their normal range of motion in order to break or dislocate bones, injure muscles, tear tendons or rip ligaments. These grappling techniques, used in martial arts such as *chin na*, *jujutsu*, Judo and Brazilian *jiu-jitsu*, force an opponent/attacker into a submissive, nonthreatening position.

Arm locks, such as the armbar, elbow lock, key lock, *juji gatame* (cross-arm lock) and shoulder lock, attempt to hyperextend, hyper-rotate or hyperflex the elbow and/or shoulder. Leg locks, such as the ankle lock, heel hook and knee bar, aim to disable the hip, knee or ankle. Small-joint manipulations twist the toes and fingers. Wrist locks rotate or hyperextend an opponent's wrist. Spinal locks, including the neck crank, can opener, cattle catch, crucifix neck crank, twister and spine crank, are the most dangerous of the joint locks.

These typically involve isolating a particular joint and leveraging it in an attempt to force the joint to move past its normal range of motion. Joint locks usually involve varying degrees of pain in the joints and, if applied forcefully and/or suddenly, may cause injury, such as muscle, tendon and ligament damage and even dislocation or bone fracture.

5.11 Biology of Conditioning

Physical fitness is an important part of martial arts training. Without a high level of core strength, cardio conditioning and mental toughness a martial artist will not be able to achieve a high level of proficiency.

Conditioning muscles

Building muscle endurance and muscle strength requires training i.e. work on endurance components of muscle fibers in targeted ways.

Muscle strength is the ability to exert a maximal amount of force for a short period (half a dozen) of time. In the gym, that may be bench pressing a heavy barbell for shorter repetitions. Muscle endurance is the ability to do something over and over for an extended period of time without getting tired. In the gym, that may be doing 5 dozen body weight squats in a row, moving to a rhythm. Muscular endurance is the ability of a muscle or group of muscles to sustain repeated contractions against a resistance for an extended period of time

Once muscles become damaged from fatigue, the body immediately attempts to repair them. This disruption activates satellite cells operating on the fringe of the muscle fibers. These satellite cells proliferate to the site of the injury and become fused together with the muscle fibers. Satellite cells add to the myofibrils, which causes them to increase in thickness and number. This is how repetition helps condition muscles.

Conditioning: Bone

One of the common ways to condition bone in martial arts is to strike a bone against another hard surface. According to Wolff's law, striking the bone causes small fractures (micro fractures) in the outer layers of the bone which are called the cortex. The layman's term for this condition is a bone bruise. The cortex of bone is comprised of small fibers which the body lays down in a kind of cross hatch pattern. It is this cross hatch pattern of fibers which then fills in with calcium to produce the strength inherent in a bon

CHAPTER 6- PSYCHOLOGICAL SCIENCE IN MARTIAL ARTS

6.1 Introduction

It's a known fact that winning a fight may not reside in one's brawn, but rather in their mind. Saying of sports psychologist Brian Cain "The best fighter never wins, it's always the guy who fights the best," very much applies in my day to day experiences. Coaches always tell that, come the fight day, the result of fight becomes a 50:50 game between mental & physical toughness. Understanding of underlying scientific concepts and key factor behind phycology of fighters is an important topic without which my study of "Science in Martial Arts" would be incomplete.

6.2 Mental Toughness

It's well-known that the stronger a fighter is mentally, the better off they are. Improving mental toughness in athletes starts by getting rid of the negativity that holds athletes back.

Negative thoughts breed negative emotions such as doubt or fear. The negativity that fighters has within themselves sets them up for a failure or impedes performance. Research has also shown that mental toughness and confidence are linked together, a positive pep talk develops positive self-talk which allows the fighters to focus on the things they can control, not the things that they can't control.

It's key that athlete's must get rid of this negative emotions to succeed. Factors like mental profile, mental imagery, feeling and mental endurance are key contributors to strengthen mental toughness which helps understand the source and cause of negative emotions.

6.3 Mental profile

This is a general architecture of the mental qualities of an athlete. Listed below are qualities that provide the mental edge, which are so important in a fight and to succeed in it.

- **Fighting spirit** – Strong spirit helps develop a strong will to fight and promotes a "don't give up "mindset.
- **Aggressiveness** – A very aggressive fighter tries to impose his will on his opponents.

- **Fearlessness** – Fighter is not afraid to receive punishment or endure pain if it helps him to have a better hand.
- **Calmness** – This allows the fighter to keep his emotions unaffected by actions.
- **Concentration** - Maintains his concentration and focus, and does not allow himself to be distracted by anything.

We'll examine these qualities and analyze their contributing factors.

Mental Profile: Fighting spirit

Fighting spirit is a key ingredient of Mental Toughness. A fighting spirit is a key mental profile which allows us to succeed in fight or life in general. It's the quality which makes us raise our head even when we're down.

Fighting spirit is extensively preached in martial arts mental training, as the "spirit to win". It is this quality which keeps us burning and motivated despite adversity.

Fighting spirit can be positively influenced by nurturing and recognizing the following soft skills:

Motivation: A feeling to excel or to achieve a goal.

Competitiveness: The competition is innate, fear of losing or surrendering: accepting mental defeat is key.

Achieving perfection: "Achieving perfection" is key motivator but often has adversarial effect. The fear of making mistakes invokes self-conscience, which if not managed may spiral into negative

Life and death situation: even a weak person are known to show amazing strength of will when dealing with life and death situation

Mental Profile: Aggressive

Being aggressive is a key strategy, although the timing of its implementation needs to be evaluated. It's the first move, execution of which may surprise the opponent thus giving advantage. It provides less time for the opponent to react.

Ultimately aggressive actions means trying to impose your will on his opponents, thus giving you control and advantage in the fight.

There are some martial arts which are not meant to be aggressive, but rather be more responsive – *"taking what your opponent gives you"* – exploiting his mistakes, instead of forcing him to make them.

Martial arts such as - Tai-chi, Aikido, and even Brazilian jiu-jitsu (especially in its traditional version, without the striking) tend to "recommend" this kind of behavior.

Mental profile: Fearless

It's a key mental profile in which a fighter is not afraid to receive punishment or endure pain if it serves his goals. Fearlessness is a usually a great virtue in a warrior/fighter, it allows him to act calmly, and rids him of the physical side effects of fear

"The difference between a coward and a hero is not fear – they both are afraid. But the coward is obedient to it, and the hero rips from its hold!"

Having fear is not wrong, not contrary it's natural. Most fighters become afraid or panic at some point, either from the fear of physical punishment or from mental strain – the thought of losing. Limited fear is not only unavoidable but necessary to perform well.

It's important to strike a balance. Being over fearless have multiple negative consequences

1. Opens to take unwanted risks, causing over confidence which may lead to lowering our guard or become over aggressive.

2. Instill feeling of numbness – a hyper feel can be generated which allows excessive adrenaline distribution causing the effect of pain to be felt less (insensitive)

Although fear is also an emotion, in a fight, it has to be managed to take advantage.

Mental Profile: Calm

To be calm to insulate actions or its impact/effect on your emotions. It is one of the most prophetically preached but very difficult to control during a fight. To bring calmness one should be able to clear of all emotions.

There are range of emotions anywhere between anger to jealousy which makes realizing calmness difficult during a fight.

• Anger usually causes over reaction, over aggressiveness

- Jealousy commonly leads to anger, but can also cause low self-esteem – resulting in insufficient aggressiveness.
- A sense of happiness – normally causes less adrenaline, and less attention.

Calmness requires controlling your inner consciousness of the brain which takes intense training such as meditation and hypnosis.

6.3.5 Mental profile: Concentrated

Maintaining one's concentration and focus is a very elementary lesson given to athletes. Quality of performance and success in fight or in general is very much related to one's ability to insulate from distraction. The focus or the state of mind is loosely referred as "in-the-zone" or "empty mind".

It is very important, to keep the mind clear, preventing any thoughts to run around in the head.

Nevertheless, the moment engagement begins during a fight or battle, we should try to clear all thoughts, this is the time to work on "auto pilot" thinking will reduce our reaction time.

6.4 Mental Imagery

A technique used by intermediate or advanced fighters in which they use their imaginations to visualize a situation and simulate the performance and feeling in that situation.

I call it a "mental warm-up", it helps to overcome nervousness and tension. In some cases, athletes can solve the problem during the imagery session while in other cases we resolve the problem afterwards with other methods.

Fighter use mental imagery during workouts to improve performance quality and review "moves" in katas. In addition, it reinforces training motivation and helps refocus on our specific workout goals. Mental imaginary is also used for relaxing and as a tool to refocus. Although it does not replace the actual practice but comes close to memorizing the steps.

Mental imagery can be invoked at various instances, in its simplest form mental imaginary is used to improve individual techniques. In this the fighter visualize the proper timing for acting i.e. visualize movement and extension of legs, hips and arms.

Mental imaginary is also used to visualize more complex moves such as all the moves and choreography associated with a kata. One can imagine performing the complete game plan or imagine the whole fight.

Mental imaginary becomes a very important tool for athletes and can be used virtually anytime, such as during training, before workout, or relaxing. Most often athletes use this before a fight. Like any technique and skill one should train it in order for it to become useful and effective.

6.5 Feelings

The practice of martial arts can be used to increase self-confidence and self-efficacy. People who are confident have learned to deal well with stress and/or dangerous situations that they have encountered through the course of their lifetime. Since the nature of martial arts is to deal with stressful situations, the practice of martial arts will increase the coping skills necessary to handle the amount of stress the person encounters (Howell, 2000). These seven coping mechanisms contribute to the development of self-confidence within the activity of martial arts. By promoting appropriate feelings, thoughts, and behaviors in martial arts training, an increase in self-confidence should be found

    Control (Howell, 2000). Control refers to the control over one's self, and is used to control thoughts, emotions, and actions (Howell, 2000). Although athletes may not have control over actual situation, but he or she can always control his or her actions, thoughts, or feelings about the situation.

    Suppression (Howell, 2000), which is the ability to deal with thoughts and emotions at the appropriate time and place (Howell, 2000). The most common emotion that a martial artist deals with is anger especially if the athlete gets punched or kicked accidentally. The instant angry reaction leads to counter attack with too much force. The martial artist must learn to suppress the feelings of anger until a more appropriate time.

    Sublimation (Howell, 2000). Sublimation is the ability to deal with negative emotions such as worry and anxiety in positive ways (Howell, 2000). Negative thoughts such as anxiety, doubt and fear are common in martial arts. One should not let these negative thoughts consume them.

Logical analysis is the ability to carefully explore problems and information in order to plan goals, answer questions, or pass along useful information (Howell, 2000). This ability especially applies to martial arts instructor, where is routinely called for problem solving.

Objectivity is the fifth major coping mechanism that can be developed through the training of martial arts (Howell, 2000). Objectivity is used to separate thoughts, feelings, and emotions in order to promote an unbiased understanding over a given situation (Howell, 2000).

Empathy is the ability to understand how a person is feeling, and how to act appropriately according to those feelings (Howell, 2000). In the martial arts, people have a tendency to establish close friendships with their training partners. They will often share thoughts and feelings with their training partners they would not be willing to share with anyone else.

Ambiguity (Howell, 2000). This is perhaps one of the most difficult coping mechanisms to develop. Tolerance of ambiguity is, "the ability to function in situations where others cannot make clear choices, because the situation is so complicated" (Howell, 2000). In these situations, the martial artists must show their ability to use all of the other major coping mechanisms in order to think and act in a correct rational manner.

Self-confidence

Theories and studies by Weinberg & Gould, 1999 in area of personality and sports phycology explains Self-confidence and its psychological traits. I have included extracts from his work.

Self-confidence can be defined as, "the belief that you can successfully perform a desired behavior" (Weinberg & Gould, 1999). Having the appropriate level of confidence is vital if one is to succeed in athletics. The appropriate level of confidence may allow athletes to concentrate more diligently on the task they are performing (Weinberg & Gould, 1999). When people are confident, they are also more likely to experience positive emotions, which in turn allow them to be relaxed and calm in the face of danger (Weinberg & Gould, 1999).

Confident people are willing to take chances because they believe in themselves and believe they will make the correct response (Weinberg & Gould, 1999). People with low levels of confidence will act more timidly, due to not believing in themselves and doubting that they will make the correct choice (Weinberg & Gould, 1999). Appropriate levels of self-confidence may also lead to increased effort in the pursuit of victory. When people feel confident, they believe in themselves and do not quit or give-up during an event when they get tired; furthermore, confident people will put forth more effort because they know they will be successful (Weinberg & Gould, 1999).

A lack of confidence is devastating to athletes and will prevent them from performing at their best because they tend to look mainly at their weaknesses; in contrast, athletes who have appropriate levels of self-confidence will focus primarily on their strengths (Weinberg & Gould, 1999).

While improving athletes' confidence level is difficult, it can be accomplished through a variety of methods. The first, and most likely the best way to increase an athlete's self- confidence is to increase the rate at which the individual successfully accomplishes their goal (Weinberg & Gould, 1999).

Overconfidence can also hinder athletes from reaching their goals and becoming their best. When people are overconfident, they have a false sense of security, and overestimate their abilities (Weinberg & Gould, 1999). Although under-confidence is usually more prevalent, overconfidence may be equally problematic.

Self-efficacy

Self-efficacy is another important factor in determining one's success. Self-efficacy is defined as "an individual's conviction that he or she can successfully execute the behaviors necessary to produce a desired outcome" (Van Raalte & Brewer, 2002).

Six major sources influence a person's self-efficacy: mastery experiences, vicarious experiences, motivation, verbal persuasion, imaginable experiences, and physiological and emotional states (Van Raalte & Brewer, 2002). The sources of self-efficacy are similar to those of sport confidence. Sport confidence and self-efficacy may go hand in hand, since both are merely extensions of state self-confidence.

Self-efficacy can influence the choice of activities a person participates in and also influences the level of effort an athlete puts forth (Weinberg & Gould, 1999). High levels of self-efficacy may lead to positive expectations in terms of sport performance (Weinberg & Gould, 1999). Positive expectations may be used to overcome psychological obstacles, such as doubt and fear of failure.

Low levels of self-efficacy can hinder performance and may keep athletes from utilizing their full potential. Although several ways to increase self-efficacy exist, perhaps the single best way to increase self-efficacy is through previous performances (Frank, 2001). Previous performances refer to past experiences a person has when he or she is performing a desired activity. The past experiences could transpire from learning and or through practice or game situations. This is why it is crucial that athletes experience success. This is also why coaches will break up complex skills into easier ones when athletes first learn techniques or movement patterns.

Self-esteem

Few studies involve the use of martial arts training to assess or improve levels of self- esteem or self-concept. Madenlian (1979) used Aikido training to see if it would improve the self-concept of the students involved in the experiment. This study shows that Aikido can be used to increase the self-confidence of 12-14 year-old students.

The authors concluded that the subjects with higher rank in Karate also had significantly higher levels of self-esteem. It was also determined that the subjects who received trophies the next day, competition winners, also had significantly higher levels of self-esteem than subjects who did not win trophies. The KTS also demonstrated that the trophy winners placed more importance on Karate in their everyday lives. This study found that people with higher self- esteem display greater ability in their sport.

Her previous research found that students with high self-esteem approach tasks with the belief that they will succeed. Gwin (1990) claims that true self-esteem means more than teaching students to feel good about themselves. She believes that students earn self-respect when they are in instructional settings that support the idea that effort will lead to success. It was hypothesized that the instruction would influence students' self-perceptions and their instructors' perceptions of their self-esteem, creating more positive self-esteem of both types.

Attitude

Attitude is related to state of mind. For some positive experiences leads to a positive attitude whereas a difficult experience can lead to negative attitude. In many case an athlete can have a fluctuating effect depending on many external or internal issues. It's always a struggle to beat the demons and consistently build a positive attitude.

Positive attitude:

Having a positive attitude in any sport, can improve your performance. By fostering emotions such as confidence and a sense of humor, you can improve your overall attitude and thus improve your proficiency.

A positive sports attitude is essential to the success of the athlete, both on and off the playing field, but it is easier said than done. During competition, it is easy to get mad about a bad play or a bad call, and it is easy to point fingers and assign blame. If that frustrated attitude and emotional state are allowed to prevail with one athlete, then that attitude will quickly become the accepted norm for the team.

What many athletes do not realize, though, is that a positive attitude is a personal choice, made every day, whether at practice or in a competition. Focus, resolve and believing in yourself go a long way a forging a positive attitude.

Negative Attitude:

Athlete's with negative attitude more often does not blossom to their potential and have negative experiences at sport. They have frustrating experience with the sport and overtime build negative self-concept. Overtime it can lead to boredom thus negatively impacting performance. Lack of commitment and resolve are common factors leading unto a bad attitude.

Encouragement and coaching can go a long way to help athlete's come out of this negative attitude.

6.6 Mental Endurance

A martial artist during a fight has not only have to endure pain, anger but also has to overcome fear and stress. Mental endurance not only prevents us from breaking, but also gives us the best mental conditions to win.

Avoiding the feeling and overcoming the obstacles are key to understanding and training for endurance.

It is now that other elements and techniques come into play and serve our mental endurance. Techniques like meditation, hypnosis, imagery and other such techniques... help us better overcome the situation and retain the focus and concentration needed.

Our endurance allows us not only to "stay in the game", but to do it in the best possible way mentally. Experience of the athlete is a big factor when building mental endurance.

6.6 Physiological Endurance & Fear - Trauma

All traumas produce an instinctive, physiological fear reaction within the human mind. Athletes past emotional or physical trauma or injury can have a severe impact on an athlete's present performances. Any worry about previous injury make the athlete nervous. As the athlete's get more and more nervous, his muscles gets automatically tight, making it impossible for him to execute smoothly and effectively.

Pain Endurance:

Pain for a martial artist can come in the form of a punch, strike, kick, or joint lock, or even a weapon. The human body contains an immense amount of nerves. Nerves are the receptors that tell the brain that some part of the body has been injured. Pain is a natural event that the body uses to warn us that we have a problem.

In a self-defense situation, being injured and dealing with the pain associated with the injury is almost a given. Pain can work for or against the victim. How one handles the pain will determine whether they can or will continue defending themselves or succumb to the assailant.

Some individuals are able to tolerate more pain than others. Whether this has to do with the environment they grew up in is one factor. The ability to tolerate pain can also be weathered through meditation or an induced self-hypnosis. Learning to raise the pain tolerance threshold is important when starting self-defense training.

The pain threshold is the point at which we perceive pain. The pain threshold in humans is fairly consistent, and pain like any other experience, is entirely a subjective. Pain tolerance is the amount of pain a person can tolerate before having to respond to it. Pain tolerance can be increased by hypnosis, medication, warmth, and strong beliefs.

Pain control and performance enhancement, are a must when training in the martial arts, and the most effective way to help oneself, is to learn self - hypnosis, hypnosis covers many areas and pain is one of the most common uses. It can influence the immune system, and is extremely good with performance enhancement, self-confidence

References for Part 2

1. http://www.louisvillemartialarts.net/pdf/pma_1.pdf

2. http://www.scienceforums.net/topic/17991-moment-of-inertia-and-martial-arts/

3. http://www.scientificamerican.com/article/the-physics-of-Karate/

4. https://thescienceclassroom.wikispaces.com/Martial+Arts+and+Newton%27s+Laws+of+Motion

5. http://entertainment.howstuffworks.com/Karate2.htm

6. http://dandjurdjevic.blogspot.com/2008/09/hitting-harder-physics-made-easy.html

7. http://www.bellaonline.com/articles/art172170.asp

8. Walker, Jearl D. "Karate Strikes." American Journal of Physics 43 (1975): 845-849.

9. https://libres.uncg.edu/ir/uncg/f/C-Matthews_Get_1997.pdf

10. http://mrobrienmmc.weebly.com/uploads/2/3/6/7/23672773/physicsofKarate.pdf

11. http://www.un.org/wcm/webdav/site/sport/shared/sport/SDP%20IWG/Chapter3_SportforChildrenandYouth(1).pdf

12. http://www.ncbi.nlm.nih.gov/pubmed/9154740

13. https://www.researchgate.net/publication/19965964_Martial_arts_injuries_The_results_of_a_five_year_national_survey

14.   Anthony T. Ngo , "An Anatomical Analysis of the weakness of the Human Body"

CHAPTER 7- CONCLUSION

It's well established that the genesis of martial arts stemmed from the need of self-defense. In the same way, it was also well understood by scholars that the development of physical resistance and building of strength not only requires conditioning one's body but also building self-confidence. This was done by enhancing chi through bolstering spiritual experiences.

My research and analysis on this subject made it abundantly clear that the grace and beauty of martial arts forms may indeed be harnessed from nature, such as from ripples of water, prowling of tigers and swagger of cobras. The generation of power and strength was an intelligent, blended use of physical, biological and psychological science. There is no doubt that the spiritual arts and physical techniques of the arts are indivisibly linked.

The true power and effectiveness of martial arts' physical techniques is firmly based on the principles of science. This study makes it clear that physics is the power behind martial arts' strength. Isaac Newton's three laws of motion easily are effectively used by the martial artists, because the three laws provide the foundation for all martial arts physical techniques. The fundamental idea is to convert potential energy from oneself or another source into your opponent efficiently.

It was fascinating to note that the techniques and styles of martial arts were well thought out and incorporated in a fundamental understanding of human anatomy and state of mind. Before a martial artist can effectively deliver powerful strikes and blocks, he must understand the anatomy of human body. Understanding of the science behind vital organs, strengths and weaknesses of the human system (skeletal, muscular, and nervous), not only allows infliction of painful punches, but also self-defense. Impact of mental states such as fear, anxiety, confidence, focus ...etc. on the human body and its performance was also noteworthy.

In the end, just as any performance requires training and practice, so does martial arts. A martial artist requires mental and physical conditioning for them to perform at their optimal Level. The training has to recognize the value of the mind, body, and spirit. Choosing which methodology of seeking spiritual enlightenment is a decision that is best left to the individual student.

Overall, it is fair to conclude martial arts cannot exist without physical science. Balancing the artistic and scientific aspects is the beauty that inspired me to write this book.

Made in the USA
San Bernardino, CA
26 December 2016